"Not very many leaders would agree to plant a church at the age of 22; even fewer would be succeeding 2 years later. In this book, Buddy uses his amazing story to take you from accomplishing your goals "someday," to starting them today."
-Carey Nieuwhof, Founding Pastor, Connexus Church
and Author of Didn't See It Coming.

"Buddy has a great story because he has lived an inspiring life! The benefit of this book is how he puts such approachable handles on living that same kind of life. Reading this book isn't just enjoyable; it's moving! Enough's enough! Start it today!"
- Clay Scroggins,
Author of *How to Lead When You're Not in Charge*
and Lead Pastor of North Point Community Church

"*Enough* will help you refocus on the goodness of Jesus and help make your "someday" plans a reality."
- Aaron Brockett,
Lead Pastor of Traders Point Christian Church

"If you've ever felt the frustration of wanting to change but not being able to, or if you've ever been tempted to give up on your dreams, on the things God has called you to do, *Enough: Someday Starts Today* is for you. Buddy has written this cogent, helpful book which will guide you through a process of letting go of your excuses and hang-ups and deciding to make 'someday' a reality today. Read it and learn from it. You'll be glad you did."
- Lane Sebring,
Author of *Preaching Killer Sermons*
and Creator of PreachingDonkey.com

"Buddy unashamedly challenges us to put away phrases that create excuses. He stirs us to make a difference with everything we've been given. This gifted leader will challenge you to use your one and only life the way it was meant to be lived. This book has made me re-evaluate my casual, someday language."
- Dan Grider,
Author of *Crucial Conversations*
and Founder of Ignite Church Network -

ENOUGH
SOMEDAY STARTS TODAY

BUDDY GOSEY

WESTBOW
PRESS®
A DIVISION OF THOMAS NELSON
& ZONDERVAN

Copyright © 2019 Buddy Gosey.

All rights reserved. No part of this book may be used or reproduced by any means, graphic, electronic, or mechanical, including photocopying, recording, taping or by any information storage retrieval system without the written permission of the author except in the case of brief quotations embodied in critical articles and reviews.

NIV: All Scripture quotations, unless otherwise indicated, are taken from the Holy Bible, New International Version®, NIV®. Copyright ©1973, 1978, 1984, 2011 by Biblica, Inc.™ Used by permission of Zondervan. All rights reserved worldwide. www.zondervan.com The "NIV" and "New International Version" are trademarks registered in the United States Patent and Trademark Office by Biblica, Inc.™
NLT: Scripture quotations marked (NLT) are taken from the Holy Bible, New Living Translation, copyright ©1996, 2004, 2015 by Tyndale House Foundation. Used by permission of Tyndale House Publishers, Inc., Carol Stream, Illinois 60188. All rights reserved.

WestBow Press books may be ordered through booksellers or by contacting:

WestBow Press
A Division of Thomas Nelson & Zondervan
1663 Liberty Drive
Bloomington, IN 47403
www.westbowpress.com
1 (866) 928-1240

Because of the dynamic nature of the Internet, any web addresses or links contained in this book may have changed since publication and may no longer be valid. The views expressed in this work are solely those of the author and do not necessarily reflect the views of the publisher, and the publisher hereby disclaims any responsibility for them.

Any people depicted in stock imagery provided by Getty Images are models, and such images are being used for illustrative purposes only. Certain stock imagery © Getty Images.

ISBN: 978-1-9736-4863-5 (sc)
ISBN: 978-1-9736-4862-8 (hc)
ISBN: 978-1-9736-4864-2 (e)

Library of Congress Control Number: 2018914744

Print information available on the last page.

WestBow Press rev. date: 01/10/2019

CONTENTS

Chapter 1   Am I Enough? 1

Trust Enough 13
   Chapter 2   Fighting Our Battles 15
   Chapter 3   Enough Faith To Question 29

Loved Enough 41
   Chapter 4   Empowered By Grace 43
   Chapter 5   Strikeout Swinging 59

Young Enough 71
   Chapter 6   What A Time To Be Alive 73
   Chapter 7   Humble And Hungry 87

Experienced Enough 105
   Chapter 8   Qualified By Our Past 107
   Chapter 9   The Dry Season Is Over 119

Called Enough 133
   Chapter 10   Hearing Well Done 135
   Chapter 11   The Danger Of Comparison 147
   Chapter 12   I Have Finished The Race 157

Acknowledgements 165
Notes 167

CHAPTER 1
AM I ENOUGH?

SOMEDAY

Someday has become the most crippling word spoken and lived in the world today. Think about it. *Someday* I will become a foster parent. *Someday* I will travel overseas to live on mission. *Someday* I will go back to school. *Someday* I will leave this rotten job. *Someday* I will lead a Bible study. *Someday* I will stop drinking. *Someday* I will start giving generously.

These commitments roll effortlessly off our tongue. We lie to ourselves and delay decisions both big and small as if *someday* will ever come. *Someday* is our favorite day. It is always close enough to enjoy as a warm thought, without ever having to feel the cold draft of discomfort that comes with change.

Someday is so toxic because it hides behind the appearance of good intentions. We settle for partial credit earned by at least considering something bold. I mean, at least we are thinking about it, right? Maybe we have even prayed a bit. But quickly we determine now is not the right time. We evaluate and convince ourselves we aren't enough, so we wait. Why would we attempt something for which we are not ready? Eventually, we will have enough experience, knowledge, money, and time, so why rush? We're still young with years ahead of us. Like a fine wine, we assume we will just become better with age. We can even justify our patient delays in a way that makes us seem wise. However, in the process, we actively have said "No" to the Creator of the universe.

I am no exception to hiding behind *someday*. The excitement of its potential is much more enjoyable than the sacrifice it would demand. *Someday* has filled slots on my calendar for years, but you know what? I'm done with it. I am ready to throw back the protective cover I've built over procrastination and expose my lack of willingness to the light, just as I would any other sin. To see this commitment through I must attack it head-on. Daily, I must go to war with my own selfish desires to shrink back and live a comfortable, mediocre life. *Someday* must die and it must die today!

Join me on a journey to discover how Jesus is enough, though we are not. Over these next twelve chapters, we will examine why we delay and then reflect on how Jesus speaks truth into the lies that have paralyzed us for too long. I pray you will read these chapters and discover how God has given you everything you need to step towards the aspirations He has put on your heart. If we allow Him, God will see us through our journey to the destination to which He called us. But, it all starts with seeing God as sufficient. We are enough, because Jesus is enough. Because of that, your *someday* can start *today*.

COUNTING THE COST

My entire life I have felt inadequate, questioning my capacity. Am I smart enough to pass organic chemistry? Do I have enough money to go to Tanzania? Do I have enough theological training to be a pastor? Am I a good enough leader to plant a church? Do I have enough life experience to write this book? Tempted to wait, to train harder, to study deeper, to earn more, I finally realized doubts have never equipped me. I have never been more thankful or in a better place after putting off the work that I knew God wanted me to do. Instead of focusing on what I don't have, I needed to shift to be in tune with what I have been given and begin stewarding that.

Now don't get me wrong, there is wisdom in preparation and realism, in counting the cost. I not only know that in my head, but believe that in my heart. Jesus even says in Luke 14,

> Suppose one of you wants to build a tower. Won't you first sit down and estimate the cost to see if you have enough money to complete it? For if you lay the foundation and are not able to finish it, everyone who sees it will ridicule you, saying, "This person began to build and wasn't able to finish." (v. 28–30)

I hate leaving something unfinished. I will give up sleep, time with my wife, and even moments with Jesus to complete a project I have started. That commitment is a blessing and a curse. It's a blessing because people can count on me to see things through. It's a curse because the fear of being known as a failure both paralyzes me from starting and consumes me once I have.

In Luke 14, Jesus speaks truth that hits home. Don't bite off more than you can chew; save the embarrassment and make sure you can finish what you started. Beyond it being humiliating not to complete a task, it depletes and wastes the time, energy, and resources we invested in the process.

Often, we respond to this caution by inaction. We think it's better to hide behind the intent of future activity than to take that first step unprepared. At first, that pause seems more noble than disobedient. The only problem is that Jesus' qualifying prerequisite to seeing the task through has nothing to do with having enough money, time or talent to finish the work He has given you. He isn't demanding we have everything together and can guarantee a successful conclusion before we commit to begin.

His point is you must have one thing, and one thing alone before you act. If you have this, you have more than enough! If you don't, you're better off waiting until you do. All other experiences, time restrictions and qualifiers come second to this.

The only thing Jesus demands of us before we start is a willingness to do whatever is asked. He says if you are willing, you are enough. In the verse before He warns us to count the cost, He drops the verbal bomb, "And whoever does not carry their cross and follow me cannot be my disciple." (v.27)

This would have shocked everyone to attention. He demanded a willing and sacrificial spirit as the primary requirement for discipleship. He demanded nothing less than willingness to pick up a cross–an instrument of torture–and carry it wherever He led them.

Jesus was saying to those gathered around Him that if they were not willing to give up control of their own lives, for the rest of their lives, they shouldn't even start the journey of discipleship! But if they are willing, nothing more is needed.

Maybe the only thing you need to ask yourself before you start your journey is whether or not you are willing to do whatever Jesus asks along the way. Are you willing to take both the first step that seems uncertain and the hundredth step that appears even more unsure? Will you follow your Good Shepherd into the valley and through the shadows? If you can commit to that, you have more than enough. God has worked with much less.

YOUNG AND RECKLESS

When you were younger, did you love to prove others wrong? We relished the opportunity to do unheard of things, to respond to dares. Granted, most of these things held no real significance, but when I was eight years old, if you told me I couldn't eat two Big Macs in one sitting or chug a whole glass of milk in six seconds, I would have jumped at the chance to prove you wrong. (Full disclosure: I did both of these! My prize was a puking up the Big Macs minutes later, much to the disgust of my mother. She used this as a teaching moment, to say the least.)

Inherent in us at a young age is a desire to show others we can do more than they believe of us. We weren't worried about accomplishing their ridiculous challenge as much as we feared missing out on the chance to try. And then something happened. We grew up and lost that spirit of challenge. We settled for ordinary.

Somehow, nearly everyone loses this adventurous spirit. Maybe it's because we gained some wisdom and realized consuming 1,200 calories of McDonald's burgers for lunch is not only awful for you, but really isn't that big of a deal. Possibly it's because the business of daily living has sucked every ounce of time and creative energy from us. But more than likely, we are stifled because the possibilities seem out of reach and we are no longer okay with trying and failing. Failure is our biggest fear and it seeps so deep we believe that it's better to play it safe. The world told us to stay in our lanes, and we listened. The enemy says we aren't qualified or ready, and before long we've lost the determination to prove him wrong. That God-given spirit that pushed us beyond our boundaries when young has been quenched. Suddenly, possibilities in daily decisions and in decade-long journeys that require mustering our imaginations to accomplish the unthinkable simply fade. We begin to enjoy hiding behind the curtain of "mature thinking."

Where in your life have you started to believe the lie that you aren't enough? Maybe you feel called to plant a church, but you don't know if you have enough experience or knowledge. Maybe you think it's time to quit your spirit quenching job and start a business, but you don't know if you have what it takes to defy those odds. Maybe that pregnancy test just came back positive, and you aren't sure if you have enough time, money or experience to raise a child. Maybe you feel you aren't enough to get married, go on a mission trip, adopt a child, stop smoking, change majors, or share your faith. Often our reliance on *someday* is a result of allowing the world instead of our Creator to define our qualifications. Luckily, God sees us differently.

LIFELONG RÉSUMÉ

As I write, my wife, Madeline, has just graduated from college and is applying to teach middle school and high school history. In a time when job openings are few, and potential candidates abound, it is easy for us to get discouraged. Even though my wife graduated from a highly respected college with a 3.8 GPA, has competitive work experience, impressive interviewing skills, and is absolutely beautiful (if I might add) she has felt like she doesn't have a chance in the arena.

Proving yourself is never fun, especially when you feel as if the person assigned to make some judgement on your potential never takes the time to truly know you. How much can someone really glean from a resume that you've been advised to keep to one page? How can the depth of your potential be explored in a 20-minute interview? Through this process, Madeline knows what it's like to be labeled by someone who doesn't truly know her.

We've been raised to work hundreds of hours just so someone can make a judgment on our abilities—our potential, our value, dare I say, our worth—in a few seconds. Graduate schools filter through hundreds of applications; potential employers will interview dozens of applicants; even getting a home loan forces you to prove yourself with a good credit score. I get it. These people only have a few hours to make a decision and under the avalanche of options they have to keep it simple.

Standardized tests, progressive work experience, debt to income ratios, and GPAs make for simple standards of measurement, signs by which to cull the herd. But you and I both know it is impossible to reveal the true, deep, capable, eager, competent, trustworthy you through a resume, test score and references from a friend. These may help paint a picture of your past, but previous achievements don't always indicate future success.

If you struggle to keep your head above water in a stream of hard and fast judgments, let me remind you of some good news.

While our world limits its concept of future potential to previous accomplishments, our God does not. The One who calls us to great things knows not only the paths we have traveled but the trails we will blaze!

God's perspective of you is not limited to what fits on one sheet of paper. He doesn't restrict us to what we can prove in a 20-minute interview. God has known us before we even spoke a word. He had plans for us before we were ever conceived. I know this because the Apostle Paul clearly tells us these facts as they apply to his own life.

> But when God, who set me apart from my mother's womb and called me by his grace, was pleased to reveal his Son in me so that I might preach him among the Gentiles… (Galatians 1:15–16)

Paul, more than anyone, knew that God is not restricted by our past to determine our future potential. God explicitly chose Paul, a murderer, liar and self-righteous religionist, to plant churches, preach the gospel to both Jews and Gentiles and write much of what became our New Testament. God could have picked a more attractive candidate with a much sweeter resume than Paul, but before Paul was even born, God had a plan for his future. This plan could never be spoiled by Paul's lack of experience, age or merit. The only thing this plan required was a willing spirit from Paul and unmeasurable grace from God to qualify him every step of the way.

Let us rejoice that God is unlimited and sees potential both in the present and in our near future—potential that a quick judgment call based on a brief resume could never discover. Jesus knew us before we were ever conceived, so of course He sees your qualifications before they are even manifest. The question is, do we trust Him enough to let Him use us as He sees us?

UTILIZING WHAT YOU DO HAVE

"Gray, Tennessee!" I quickly exclaimed. I had spent plenty of time thinking and praying about where we might plant a church and I didn't need another moment to consider it. This was a no-brainer to me. Gray was just miles from my hometown of Johnson City, it had a rising number of unchurched millennials and our North Ridge Community Church network didn't have a presence there.

As I explained my reasoning to our lead pastor, Jim Richmond who had just asked me where I wanted to help lead our next church plant, the weight of the challenge ahead started to hit me. I had just agreed not only to pastor a church but to plant one from the ground up. Hearing my enthusiastic and reasoned response to the opportunity, Jim smiled and agreed. Gray was his hometown, and he couldn't be more excited to entrust me, a 21-year old punk at the time, with starting a movement that could turn that community upside down.

There were many moments both before and after that summer morning in 2015 that I doubted if we could really plant a growing church with me as the pastor and leader. I still had two semesters left of undergraduate studies in Food Science and Technology at UT-Knoxville. We had no money and no core group. I had little experience preaching and even less training in theology and leadership.

It would have been easy to focus on all I lacked and to wonder if I was enough. I started to think, "Surely God would have an easier time using someone else," as if God needed some help in His decision making and did not enjoy a good challenge.

Luckily, God did not let me dwell in doubt for too long. Every time I began to feel choked out by inadequacy, God sweetly reminded me of what He had provided. And trust me, it was more than enough.

First, I had the Holy Spirit. The same power that raised Christ from the dead and started a movement that has lasted 2,000 years was not only alive in me, but working in the lives of those around me. That alone is enough.

But on top of that, I had support from an amazing group of church leaders throughout the North Ridge Network. They saw both my work ethic and my heart for the Kingdom of God and didn't make me prove myself further for my chance to step into more. I am forever indebted to the willingness of Jim Richmond and North Ridge Community Church to see me as God sees me, a young man who was willing. They believed in me, and I knew I would always have their support.

Lastly, I knew how to makes disciples and felt that if I could empower a small group of people to do that with me, this couldn't fail. When I took a step back and saw all God had entrusted to me, I realized I had more than enough, and it was time to get to work. That's precisely what I did.

Over the next 10 months, I coasted through my senior year of college and focused on preparing the foundation for our church plant. God provided over $30,000 in start-up funds and a core group of 25 underqualified but willing disciple makers and leaders. He gave us a building to rent that I would not invite my worst enemy to live in, but we made it our home.

Most importantly, the Lord imbued us with confidence in His goodness that helped us step out of the boat and into the storm ahead, just as Peter did a couple of thousand years earlier. (Matthew 14:29)

As we moved into core group meetings and toward a public launch, God began to grow me as a leader as He built His church. I experienced how much you grow as you go. I saw how my mistakes can become valuable lessons. I witnessed God's ability to redeem my mistakes into something beautiful.

Three years after that initial conversation with Jim, we still haven't accomplished the goal of seeing our entire community transformed…yet. But we have seen Jesus change lives. We have witnessed young men start to follow Jesus and then baptize their best friend just months later. We have seen underqualified leaders emerge who once had no idea how much God could use them if they were merely willing.

We've outgrown our first building and are quickly outgrowing our second. Young millennials not only are attending, but are becoming disciple makers. Of course, there is much work to do, but that excites me because as our church grows, I get to grow as a leader.

I will never claim to have it all figured out. Instead, I will boast that I am "underqualified" and "too young," for as long as I can because I know God is qualifying me as I go. Besides, I would rather be labeled "too young" to do something and grow into it, than to stand on the sideline and watch it pass.

This 24-year-old pastor and church planter with a bachelor's degree in food science, could not be more confident that he is exactly where God wants him to be. Because of that, I will press on into the unknown.

QUALIFYING THE CALLED

I've always been told that "God doesn't call the qualified, He qualifies the called." I've always wondered, though, how He accomplishes that. I didn't disagree with the statement, I just wanted to know how it happened. I would think, "Here I am God, clearly unqualified, get to qualifying." After not hearing audibly from God, I did pick up a few things about how He works in this qualifying process, as well as how to get the most out of it.

I've realized this: qualification isn't as much about doing more to get ready, as it is recognizing what's already been done for you. It isn't about accumulating credentials or experiences, as much as developing a willing spirit to say "yes" and trust God to equip you as you go.

Qualification requires you to reject labels that the world sticks on you so you can accept the title given by your Creator. Could it be that the very thing we are doing to qualify—waiting—is actually the only thing that takes our qualification away?

I don't know what Jesus is pushing you toward. Maybe you aren't even sure. But when He makes it clear, whether big or small, I encourage you to set a deadline and start to make it happen. Your *someday* may not be accomplished today. It may not even be tomorrow. But a sure way to see your *someday* aspiration never happens is by letting it remain *someday*. Replacing *someday* with *this day* is the first step to becoming qualified to do God-sized things. So embrace that goal. Pick a deadline. Start acting on it now!

God wants you to arrive at the destination He's planned for you. The journey may not be what you expect. Unforeseen challenges might pop up, but don't let that stop you. Count the cost, confess your willingness and start now!

Join me on this journey to discover what it takes to see your *someday* aspirations through. I hope this book will help you begin to believe that you are enough to do great things because you have a God who is enough to do abundantly more than you could think or imagine. (Ephesians 3:20)

Take a moment right now and confess to God where you feel underqualified. Confess the times such a thought has kept you from being willing to follow Jesus where He is leading you. Be honest and talk to Him about your fear of failure and the discouragement you have endured.

Now take your eyes off yourself and your past, and fix them on Jesus and His future plans for you. The good news is, we are not fighting this upward battle alone. We have a mighty warrior named Jesus who is with us every step of the way.

ASK YOURSELF:

- Am I willing to take up my cross and follow Jesus wherever He leads? If not, what keeps me from being willing?

- Do I believe a willing spirit is the most important qualifier for getting started?

- To what have I said *someday* that God wants me to start today?

- How have previous disappointments and labels stuck on me by others quenched the childlike, adventurous spirit I once had?

- Do I believe God is able to qualify me as I go? If I did believe it, how would this change the way I approach God-given opportunities?

PART 1
TRUST ENOUGH

CHAPTER 2
FIGHTING OUR BATTLES

WILLING TO FIGHT

A few summers ago I said yes to investing a couple of weeks of my life in Tanzania with a ministry called the Jesus Film Project. Not knowing exactly what I would be doing or how to find the $3,000 needed to go, my excitement prompted me to commit. To no surprise, God did not disappoint.

In Tanzania—farther than I'd ever traveled—I stepped into a whole new world. Our mission was simple: to tell as many people as we could about Jesus and the life change He brings. Every afternoon, our 20-member team split into groups of five and traveled to a rural village to show The Jesus Film which had been translated into the local language.

To be honest, The Jesus Film is not something I typically would sit and watch on a Friday night. It was filmed in the 1970's and looks like something that airs before sunrise on public television in the South. I feel no guilt about making light of the film's age and production values, because I would never deny its effectiveness! This two-hour production accurately visualizes the gospel of Luke and shares the entire life and life changing, good news of Jesus. Children and adults alike were mesmerized to see a movie and to hear this man named Jesus speak as if He were talking to them directly.

After taking a couple of days to adjust our psyche to an entirely new world, we fell into a simple, yet effective routine. Every afternoon we would head to a local village and set up the projector. Then, we'd walk around the village, and use our broken Swahili to invite everyone to join us for the film showing at sunset. We typically had enough time for me to get dominated by some eight-year-olds in soccer before heading back to the projector for show time.

These were some of the best nights of my life. Laying in the back of a truck, beneath a blanket of stars so thick I thought for the first two nights it was fog. Every night I cried out to the Father for hours, begging Him to change lives. And let me tell you, He did! After the film, we shared our life change stories and invited people to confess Jesus as their Lord and Savior and follow Him. Every night I would get to pray with dozens of new believers and celebrate the lost being found.

After we connected the new believers with a local pastor, we went home to rest for the night. In a region where over 95 percent of the people practiced Islam or native witchcraft, we saw the Spirit of God flow in and raise new hope. That week, thanks in part to work done in advance by local pastors, more than 1,000 people professed faith in Jesus, we helped to fortify dozens of churches and to start six new churches. To this day, I am beyond thankful that God helped make that *someday* aspiration into a reality. All I had to do was say "yes" and follow Him.

Toward the end of the first week, I remember saying, "I cannot believe how easy this is!" God prepared the hearts of these people before we arrived. They were ready for a new hope and all we had to do was obediently share it. East African hospitality was something I had never experienced. Their smiles and affection were good for the soul and made us feel like we belonged. Because of that, a part of my heart remains there.

Perhaps the biggest surprise was how safe I felt. Most of the time I felt safer in the darkness of night, halfway across the world, than I did in my own neighborhood in Tennessee. You could not ask for anything more. Everything went better than planned. Except for one night. That night I experienced fear in a way I've not experienced since.

As soon as we got out of the truck, we knew that night would be different. Without having to say a word, everyone shifted to high alert. On this night we were much closer to the city and nearly 1,000 people milled around, as opposed to the usual 300-400 in the villages. Unlike other nights, the majority of people weren't children, but adults. To top it off, many of those coming up to us were heavily intoxicated, and not the "friendly" type of drunk if you know what I'm saying.

As we set about getting our program and projector in place, threatening looks pierced the air. Confrontational shouts were lobbed at us from every direction. Even though we didn't speak the language, we knew what they were saying solely by their tone. In addition to a massive culture gap that made communication for an American like myself nearly impossible, our own translator couldn't even understand many of the men as cheap liquor covered their breath and impeded their speech.

As the screaming and gesturing continued and some of our possessions were being carried away in the arms of thieves, my open-handed posture to God began to close into fists of defense. To top it all off, we were very undermanned that night. Every other night we traveled with a group of five Americans and a couple of local pastors. For whatever reason, we thought it would be a good idea to go with only me, my friend Cole, two American women and a local Tanzanian woman of faith that evening. We had little physical presence as our average body weight did not come close to 150 lbs.

I am usually a "talk it out" kind of guy. I have a pretty good stature and can hold my own, but I am not the type to throw a punch, and I wasn't feeling too good about getting my first fight night experience while a Christian guest in a rural African village. If it came down to fight or flight, we were ready to sprout wings.

To this day, I don't know why that milling crowd wanted us to leave, but I will never forget the distress I felt that evening. As our team discussed whether or not we should return to camp, we decided to call in and wait for backup. For the next 20 minutes, we waited, defenseless, every one of us on high alert.

Paralyzed and confined to our small huddle, we didn't dare set up our equipment. We prayed, and got more and more nervous about staying. I was ready to cut our losses and live to show The Jesus Film another day. Besides, if they were hostile, they weren't going to listen to our message anyway. My mind ran wild with doubts.

At the height of my distress, everything suddenly grew eerily silent. I looked up and saw the crowd split in half as if God had just parted the Red Sea yet again. The driving wedge that caused the division was four tall men, draped in traditional African garb. They walked directly into and through the crowd, their mere presence commanding respect. Each with a six-foot staff in hand and a machete at their side, these imperturbable men walked up and simply stood by our truck. The Maasai had arrived.

We had seen Maasai men throughout the week and knew their reputation from the locals. Maasai are semi-nomadic tribesmen from Tanzania and Kenya, historically fierce warriors once required to kill a lion as their rite of passage into manhood. Though that practice is now illegal because of the decline in lion population, the reputation and swagger they gained with being labeled lion killers still clings to them. Maasai also are unusually tall. As they approached our truck I saw that each of these slender men were a head taller than the people around them. Yet, it was not their height or weapons that commanded respect. These men were warriors, and unlike me, they came ready to fight.

To this day, I cannot recall if these Maasai men ever spoke a word to us. I do remember that all of them, solemn-faced and serious, stood firmly in front of our truck and equipment. They clearly were there for us. Our translator whispered to me, "They will protect us." After a few more minutes of hesitancy, my closed fists began to relax open again as the rowdy crowd started to disperse. About ten minutes later we were able to get back to setting up the film. That night, nearly a thousand people watched The Jesus Film. That night, Jesus changed lives.

After the film started, I climbed into the back of the truck and began to talk to my Father. Gazing up at the brilliant Milky Way, I had a sense of confidence and peace knowing I had someone ready to fight for me. Worship displaced fear. I smiled as God's Spirit reminded me of Exodus 15:3, "The LORD is a warrior; the LORD is his name."

That night, God showed me He is a warrior who fights my battles for me. Under those stars, I experienced the peace that comes when resting under the protection of a warrior. Any time fear tried to creep into me during that tense hour, I merely had to gaze at the tall men next to me who at any moment were ready and willing to fight. God fights our battles for us. That night He did so by sending four of his best to protect His servants.

We experience fear when we take our eyes off of the powerful One who fights our battles. When you keep your vision locked onto your strong defender, insecurity is swept away. As impressive and able as were the Maasai, how much more of a warrior do we have in Jesus? A warrior who not only can wield a rod, staff or machete against our enemies, but who is the very creator of the materials needed to make them.

Much like that starry night in Africa, whenever fear creeps up our spine and the crippling commotion of the world buzzes in our ears, we need to take our eyes off of our circumstances and gaze directly on the warrior who is willing to fight for us. We may be in the presence of our enemies, but our shepherd-warrior Jesus comforts and protects (Psalm 23). Our confidence should never waver because our protection never depends solely on our own abilities. Let our courage always come from Him.

HAVE NO FEAR

If success depends entirely on our qualifications, the Bible is a book of lies. Abraham, Moses, David, Daniel, Mary and Matthew are all people I'd never pick for my team, but God did and He molded them into champions. The entire history of God's people is littered with individuals who—when He chose them—were too young, uneducated, inexperienced and sinful to make a difference. They would have a hard time getting a job at your local supermarket yet God chose them to lead a nation, plant churches and parent the Savior of the world. They may not have had the credentials, but they were willing to trust God to equip them as they go. They believed the Lord would fight their battles and make them into "enough," when the trials came. He would see them through. Perhaps my favorite example of this is found in the prophet, Jeremiah.

Jeremiah was called to be a prophet to Judah and the nations when he was younger than 20 years old—just a teenager[1]. As you can imagine, Jeremiah at first wasn't sure God had the right guy. But the Lord reassured him, as he records in Jeremiah 1:4–5, saying, "The word of the Lord came to me, saying, 'Before I formed you in the womb I knew you; before you were born I set you apart; I appointed you as a prophet to the nations.'"

God has plans for us, amazing plans, initiated before we even were born. We worship a Creator who knew us before we were formed in the womb. He is a designer, a builder and creator who installed tools and capabilities in us we've never discovered because we haven't opened our control center to Him. Even though most of us aren't called as prophets to the nations, each of us has been set apart uniquely. Do you believe that? Do you believe God has set you apart for something unique and meaningful?

As different as our plans may be, they have one thing in common. Success will require more than our own abilities. An obedient response to God's call on your life will always require to seek more of Him. Prayer will no longer be an afterthought as you must beseech God to show up in a big way. Trusting in yourself alone is off the table because you know you no longer are enough. You won't be able to give yourself credit for whatever is achieved because it's so massive, only God could be responsible.

A sense of holy fear will naturally wash over you when you live totally dependent on God. Suddenly, you are relying 100 percent on someone you can't see, but believe will be there. You trust you will be able to discern what God wants, even though you've never heard His voice. Jeremiah felt these same natural fears. He realized he was being asked to do something for which he wasn't qualified. As you may expect, doubt slapped him in the face as this young man considered the weight of expectations on his young life.

> "Alas, Sovereign Lord," I said, "I do not know how to speak; I am too young." But the Lord said to me, "Do not say, 'I am too young.' You must go to everyone I send you to and say whatever I command you. Do not be afraid of them, for I am with you and will rescue you," declares the Lord. (Jeremiah 1:6–7)

When I first read this, I thought Jeremiah was one lucky dude. He heard the audible voice of God, so he could live without doubt of what God wanted. He would go down in history as one of God's chosen prophets. Not only that, he would have power to perform miracles and be guided by God in a way no ordinary person would. That's a no-brainer. Sign me up!

But before you focus on all the perks, consider the weight of what God just asked Jeremiah to do. He is to be a messenger to both Judah and to the nations on which God's anger and wrath will fall. He gets to proclaim messages of hope, but only after declarations of judgment. As you can imagine, those words aren't always well received.

By this point in his life, Jeremiah knows the fantastic things earlier prophets have accomplished as well as the rejection they faced. Many lived in fear from those to whom they brought the word of God. Some were hunted down and stoned. Jeremiah had a lot to be concerned about. Given the not-so-glamorous life of a faithful prophet, he mutters a legitimate excuse. "Not Me God, I am too young."

When we feel called by God to a task, too often we think first of what likely will go wrong. We run a quick cost-benefit analysis and our initial willingness gets eased aside with an excuse. Scholars believe Jeremiah was between 17 and 20 years old, so his hesitancy based on age may be more a legitimate response than a cop out.

We, too, are great at offering God solid excuses, as if He didn't know our age, experience or abilities before He chose us. We immediately remind God that we can't quit our job because we don't have enough savings or we shouldn't welcome that needy person to live in our home, because we just got married. We find great ways to inform God that we just had a child so we can't travel overseas or we're about ready to retire, so going back to school makes no sense.

I appreciate Jeremiah's honesty. I think God does too. We must be honest with God, because it is only when we are honest with Him that He can replace all of these man-made reasons with one God-given truth, "I am with you and will rescue you."

The beauty of serving a sending God is that when He sets us apart He goes ahead of us every step of the way. He shoulders the struggle with us. He doesn't erase our excuses, but understands they might be reasonable concerns that lead to hesitation. However, God won't waste time supporting your "rationalizations". Instead, He'll expose them as lies with the light of the truth that He is our warrior, and He is enough. God crushes obstacles of age, experience, or finances under the weight of one promise: He will be with you. He will rescue you when your excuses become real-life challenges, and trials threaten your confidence.

God never promises us an easy journey. He will never cheat you of the growth opportunities that lie in the challenges ahead. But amongst these obstacles, He flexes His abilities the most. It is under the protection of this one promise—that He is with you—that 99 excuses are washed away.

Although we aren't called to exclaim, "Thus says the Lord"

and be a prophet as Jeremiah was, each of us has been set apart for ministry. These ministries will change and grow over time, and it is our responsibility to respond when God gives the opportunity.

Jeremiah started his ministry as a priest, certainly a worthy calling. But can you imagine if he settled for a sedate life in the Temple over the next 50 years? He would have missed out on so much!

Where in your life have you settled and never stepped toward the "something more" to which you felt called? Jeremiah saw his service as a priest was good but knew there was more. He rejected fear, and responded to God's call.

We, too, get the chance to renounce fear and say "No" to settling for good. Sometimes fear arrives in the form of drunk Africans. Other times it manifests in concern for what people might think of us. If some of our fears are legitimate concerns, others are merely excuses. The fact is, our fears result from being too focused on ourselves and the limits of our own abilities. Fear cripples us from walking in the truth of who God is! We doubt we are enough instead of proclaiming that He is. The moment we believe God is enough, we will be able to say "No" to good, and "Yes" to God. We will exclaim as the psalmist did in Psalm 118:6, "The Lord is on my side; I will not fear. What can man do to me?"

No person, self-doubt, or limitations should cause us to hesitate. Nothing is too hard for the Lord! Do you believe that? Does your life reflect that? Does the last year of your life affirm that? Or have you settled for a life of mediocrity, comfort and constancy? The God who makes demons tremble quiets our own fright as He stands by our side. With God on our side, we have nothing to fear. We will always have enough and can be enough.

ABUNDANT BLESSINGS

Pretty regularly we will come to a point in our lives where we feel we lack enough time, knowledge, physical ability or money to do the things we feel led to do. In this space, we can do two things. We can wait, and ask God for a little more of whatever we feel we lack; or, we can give everything we have at present and be forced to desperately beg Jehovah Jireh to provide.

Before you slide into that *someday* mentality and are tempted to hoard God's blessings, let me remind you of life-altering good news. We serve a God who not only is able to bless us when we need more, but gives abundantly when we need it most.

> And God is able to bless you abundantly, so that in all things at all times, having all that you need, you will abound in every good work. (2 Corinthians 9:8)

You cannot out give God! You just can't do it. The One who spoke the world into being is overjoyed to provide us with every blessing. However, notice that Paul says God is "able". Many times I read God's word and wish just a word or two was different. Why not say "God will bless you" or that God "already has blessed you." Instead, Paul reminds us that we can experience God-sized things—He is able—but God distributes His graces only as He sees fit and as needed for good works to abound in our lives.

We would all love to receive the benefits of God's promises before the act of obedience occurs. We want the trophy before we run the race. But God won't settle for that. Throughout His Word, the promise is always conditional to the command. Proverbs 3:6 promises to make our paths straight. I love that promise in times where I feel I lack direction. But to receive this promise, God commands we first trust in Him with all of our heart, refuse to lean on our own understanding, and acknowledge Him in all our ways.

Sounds easy right? Nope! Any one of those things is hard, but three of them together is nearly impossible. Why can't God just show me where to go? He's the cosmic GPS, the ultimate Google Maps. Why must I jump through all those hoops first? Why can't I receive the blessing before the obedience?

We would all love to be blessed before we act. We could even reason that a lot more could get accomplished if the blessing was up front. The good news is that God never settles for what we think is best. God knows the blessing is only the whipped topping on our dessert. The real substance, the fudge brownie with ice cream, is the faith we grow in the process of receiving the blessing through faithful obedience. To invest deeply in God with all we have, to go through the battles and see our Warrior defend us, to meet the challenges and experience the joy of obedience is God's ultimate desire for us. That's where we acquire deep seated, sustaining faith. In these moments when fear begins to grip us because we have nothing left to offer, we learn to trust. True dependence is exhibited as you hold nothing back and realize if He doesn't provide abundantly, you won't be able to continue. You now have nowhere to turn except God. You have completely stripped away all safety nets. Holding nothing back is where we gain freedom through total dependence on God's providence to continue.

I will never forget Jim Richmond, our North Ridge Network leader, telling me that he wants to live and lead in a way that so depends on God, that if God doesn't come through, he looks like a fool. Since then, I've tried to adopt that mindset. I want to give everything I have and put myself in situations where my all isn't enough, where I will look foolish if God's "enough" doesn't make up for my insufficiency. When you come to this place, blessings are sure to follow. God loves to give you all you need to abound in good works! Your insufficiencies will disappear under a flood of abundance to reassure you He is more than you could ever need. In this place of utter dependence, you focus more on who God is than on anything He will give—more on the Giver, than on the gifts.

I am thankful that God would rather grow my faith than my fat. He knows more than a little extra food in my belly, knowledge in my head, or money in my pocket, I need to learn to trust Him actively. When I do I get both! I get the gift and the Giver.

There is no guarantee that we will get what we want when we

want it. But, there is a better promise. A promise of God blessing us abundantly how and when He sees best to allow us to abound in every good work. Often the abundant blessings we need only occur to a depleted servant who has given up everything. It is when we have exhausted, every ounce of energy, every dollar in our savings, and every creative thought in our minds, that our Master gives us back the things we have given Him, plus so much more.

In this space of utter dependence for more, a shift occurs. We no longer ask for more merely to spend it on us, but begin pleading for an abundance so we can steward it and give it right back to God. We just want to experience being a part of His plan and provision. In this space we become so laser-focused on the joy of encountering God's grace, we forget about any gain for ourselves. We can't wait to immediately spend every God-given gift on the good works He has for us so we can once again be depleted and dependent on Him. We become addicted to the thrill of seeing how our Heavenly Father provides just as Jesus promises He will in Matthew 7.

> If you, then, though you are evil, know how to give good gifts to your children, how much more will your Father in heaven give good gifts to those who ask him! (Matthew 7:11)

Our confidence swells when we give all we have and see God respond in abundance with all that we need. We reject saving God's blessings for another day because we want to see what He can do with it now as we enjoy watching Him provide. We know that ultimately more will be needed in the future, but the provision required can only be obtained by laying down the little we currently have at the feet of Jesus. What we have to offer is enough. When we need more, it will be given to us, but only after we give our all.

Let us abound in every good work, knowing that our Father loves to give abundantly to His children who are exhausted from giving Him everything.

ASK YOURSELF:

- Am I living a life that is actively dependent on God?

- Do I recognize that I need Him with me every step, to be my warrior and fight my battles? Do I trust that He not only sets me apart but will see me through?

- How can I grow my dependence and trust in the Lord?

- Where in my life have I settled for good and never taken that next step into something more?

- Where have I been faithful in the past, but may be hesitating about what God wants for me next?

- Am I genuinely dependent on God at this moment? Have I put myself in a position that if God doesn't come through, I am in trouble?

CHAPTER 3
ENOUGH FAITH TO QUESTION

A DESPERATE FATHER

It is a warm afternoon in Galilee. Jesus, Peter, James and John search for the rest of the disciples so they can get back to Capernaum after a long and emotional day on the mountain. Then, the lingering crowd spots Jesus and flock to Him. Some vie for His undivided attention, others just want to get near enough to touch His robe.

In the chaos, Jesus finally finds the rest of His disciples. As He approaches, He notices some sort of disagreement developing. The local religious leaders have stuck their noses in someone else's business yet again and are tearing down the disciples for their lack of effectiveness. Although He is exhausted, Jesus takes advantage of the teaching moment at hand and asks what the dispute is about.

Before any disciple or religious leader can mutter a word, a frail voice from the crowd musters every ounce of energy and faith he has to explain the situation. This father steps forward to say his son is possessed by a demon and for years has been mute and epileptic. He says he has done everything he can to find Jesus' disciples in the hope they could cure him, but they have fallen short. His son continues to have seizures.

Jesus' response is one you'll often read in scripture, and I don't blame Him. He wonders aloud how long He has to put up with this unbelieving generation. I'm not sure if He's more frustrated with the religious leaders or His own disciples, but he acquiesces to the father's pleas, and has him bring his son forward.

When the boy comes to Jesus he is immediately seized by another convulsion. As he rolls around on the ground, foaming at the mouth, Jesus calmly asks the father how long this has been going on. "Since he was a child," the father exclaims, fearfully. He then adds that the demon has tried to kill the boy for years by throwing him into water or fire with these attacks.

At this point, the father can't wait any longer. He's at the end of his rope, desperate for action. He is exhausted from anxiety and the sleepless nights he's endured to keep his son safe. The money he's spent going from doctor to rabbi to doctor, seeking answers with no success, has left him broke and broken. He takes one more look at his scar-covered son, foam erupting from his mouth, and with his last ounce of hope and faith, cries out to Jesus, *"But if you can do anything, take pity on us and help us."* (Mark 9:22)

The son's illness has whittled the man's faith until it is weak as a splinter. Knowing this, Jesus seizes the opportunity to not only physically heal a son, but spiritually restore a broken father. This father needs a fresh reason to believe.

At the story's apex, Jesus turns the arch. Instead of simply healing, He criticizes the father. The Savior of the world responds to this desperate plea with a question of his own. *"If you can? Everything is possible for one who believes."* (v.23)

Jesus knew the only way to grow this man's faith was to make him exercise every ounce of it. He would settle for nothing less. At this critical moment, the father could go home with his tail between his legs, embarrassed, exhausted, and defeated, or he can try again. He can be bold enough to demonstrate his faith one last time. He has worked for weeks, maybe months to find and finally stand before the one man who he hopes can help his son. At this crossroad, the father assumes a position of humility, humility that produces a confession.

His confession—leaping off the pages of scripture—has changed my life forever. He confesses something I bring to Jesus as often as I can, a confession we need to exclaim in the dark to find God more often. Verse 24 tells us that upon hearing Jesus' response, the father immediately confesses, *"I do believe; help me overcome my unbelief!"*

The father audaciously reminds Jesus of his belief! A substantial amount of belief, if I may add. The faith required to drag your demon possessed child around all day in the desert heat, exposing him to ridicule in a large crowd of strangers, is staggering. That level of humiliation he is willing to endure as a function of his faith goes far beyond the too familiar Walmart meltdowns that terrorize parents of misbehaved children. The man knows he believes. Jesus knows he believes. But the humility to admit his belief is incomplete and needs help is unheard of.

The boy's father doesn't just need help, he wants it. He trusts Jesus enough to ask for it. He doesn't know what else to do but be honest. He now has asked not only for a demon-free child but also a renewed faith. I think Jesus knew the latter was just as important as the first.

This confession of unbelief has become my life prayer. If one statement describes my faith journey, it is that of faith mixed with unbelief. I believe Jesus is my Savior. I believe He is good and is on my side. I believe He has a plan for my life and will make a way. I believe He provides.

But when I am honest with myself, I confess there are times I don't believe fully. I question if He answers my prayers. I sometimes even doubt He is in control of my life, or the lives around me.

Often I don't trust that He is good enough to prompt me to action. If faith without works is dead, as the book of James says, what does that say about my level of unbelief when I shrink away from the works God has laid out for me? So yes, there are times I don't believe Jesus is enough. I am okay confessing that because I know

Jesus is good news to all of my unbelief. He is the only one who can help me overcome it. Like the possessed boy's father, I know it is only when I have faith enough to trust Him with this confession that I receive the help I need.

UNBELIEVABLY GOOD NEWS

The reason it is so hard to believe the good news of who Jesus is, what He has done, and what He promises to do, is because it is unbelievably good! This may be a rare case where the too-often used expression "unbelievable" is appropriate! For our entire life we've been taught to perform to be accepted. School, work, sports, relationships, band and even drama club all demand our best. Since we were children, we've received the message that if we don't perform well, we will be rejected, criticized, and left disappointed by the people we trusted the most.

After years of overworking, being anxious to please, and still being let down, we begin to project the actions of the people around us onto God. We think we have to perform to be accepted by Him. Could it really be there is a perfect Creator who can tell us to stop working harder and just come enjoy Him? Does God really accept us when we are at our worst because of the sufficient sacrifice of Christ? Does He really have a hope and a future for us even when we've gone off script? It sounds way too good to be true.

Our parents, coaches, friends, co-workers and mentors have done nothing but over-promise and under-deliver our entire lives. Why should we stick our necks out, just to add God to the list of those who disappoint us? We'd rather never believe the goodness of the Gospel than run the risk of trusting it and being let down again.

As hard as it may be, we must fight to believe just how unbelievably good the Gospel is. *The Gospel is God's story restoring our story.* It's the truth that God loved us enough to send His Son to take the punishment for our sins so that all who believe in Jesus as their Lord and Savior can become holy, spotless, pure, children of God forever. It may be hard for you to grasp the ramifications of this good news but you must wrestle with it. It's a matter of life and death.

God doesn't wait to restore our story until after we die. He begins redeeming it the moment we trust Him to be enough. Sadly, it seems easier to trust God with our eternity than with our current life. We trust Jesus to save us from hell but aren't sure He can sustain us on earth. We know Jesus is sufficient to cover our sin, but doubt He will be enough to show up in our day-to-day. We know we are forgiven enough to go to heaven someday, but we're not confident He accepts us enough that we dare to confess unbelief today.

We can quote scripture and spout Christian lingo about redemption, righteousness and justification as future milestones. But too many of us don't believe those things change our lives now. We are to be pitied if we speak like Christians without allowing the truths of what Christ has done to transform us.

Paul writes in Romans 8:32 how the Gospel should charge us with confidence today: "He who did not spare his own Son, but gave him up for us all—how will he not also, along with him, graciously give us all things?" If God gave you something as precious as his Son, why would He withhold anything you need in the now? He enjoys giving! One reason that boldness marked Paul's life is that He knew Jesus changes our daily life, not just our afterlife. The same God who loves us enough to send His Son to cover our sins will send us enough to meet our needs. Paul lived a life that allowed the gospel not only to save his soul, but to change his life. The truth of Jesus' life gave him confidence that this unbelievably good news actually was believable. Because of that, he was never the same.

During my entire Christian walk I've struggled to ensure I never move past the Gospel, but merely deeper in my understanding of it. I sometimes convince myself I entirely understand this life-changing truth, when in reality I've only scratched the surface. As I've grown in my knowledge of doctrine and theology, one simple fact resounds within me: *when I am not enough, Jesus is*. If Jesus can overcome the grave, He can surely help me overcome my unbelief. Not only can He help, He wants to help! Jesus invites your unbelief and when you confess it, He shows He is worthy of all your belief. He is good news to all of my unbelief and He can be good news to you too.

All of us are unbelievers. Some more frequently than others, but even those who trust in God and follow Jesus have periods, moments or seasons of unbelief. Even the legends of our faith questioned God. In addition to Jeremiah and this unbelieving father in Mark 9, Moses, Joshua, Job, David, John the Baptist, and even Jesus questioned God. And guess what, God disqualified none of them for their unbelief.

Each and every one of them went on to do miraculous works! It was as if their questions moved them toward action rather than giving unexpressed doubts a foothold to paralyze and cripple them. Maybe the only thing keeping us from stepping into the upward calling that God has for us is our own inability to trust God enough to question Him.

CHILD-LIKE QUESTIONS

Children love to ask questions. Their humility and curiosity to learn is beautiful in many ways. It's also very annoying. Don't judge me, you know it's true. We've all been sucked into the black hole of their never-ending innocent questions. That curious four-year-old's one question quickly becomes five with a few "why's?" and a couple "how's?" that force from you an unending litany of explanations. Luckily, I've become a pro at shutting them down. Shame me all you want, I just don't feel the need to explain everything.

Here is some free advice. The best way to shut down the merry-go-round of questions is to give them a taste of their own medicine. Respond to every question of theirs with a question of your own. Try it! Match every "why?" with a "why not?" It works!

It also worked for Jesus, except I think His motives were much more pure than mine. As annoying as it can be to try continually to satisfy a kid's curiosity, think about the heart of a child. Children don't question because they doubt. They ask because they just want to know, and they trust you to have some answers. Children possess humility and trust, both of which are needed to seek truth. We could learn a lot from them.

Our Heavenly Father loves to reveal truth, and to give us wisdom and understanding. Luckily, unlike me, God is not easily annoyed or impatient. He has all the time in the world, and He wants to spend it with us, even if we ask the same simple questions over and over. James 1:5 tells us that, "If any of you lacks wisdom, you should ask God, who gives generously to all without finding fault, and it will be given to you." We can question God because He loves revealing truth to His children! He desires to hold nothing back. David Guzik explains it like this:

> Knowing God's generosity—that He never despises or resents us for asking for wisdom—should encourage us to ask Him often. We understand that He is the God of the open hand, not the God of the clenched fist.[1]

However, you should know there is one prerequisite before bringing our questions to God. God demands we question within the borders of faith. Our questions should be motivated by the desire to grow closer to Jesus. We should assume He will reveal truth. James explains it like this in James 1:6, "But when you ask, you must believe and not doubt, because the one who doubts is like a wave of the sea, blown and tossed by the wind."

Our Father is thrilled when we come before Him like a child. He delights in our confidence that we can depend on Him for an answer and is pleased when we trust the new truths He reveals. Just as a son approaches his father, expecting his daddy to help, we come to our Heavenly Father when we lack understanding, sure that our *Abba* will meet us where we are and be thrilled to spend time sharing truth.

I don't think it is realistic to live a life free of questioning. An aspect of unbelief will always live in the midst of our faith. Hip hop artist Andy Mineo put it like this: "The opposite of faith ain't doubt. It's when I got it all figured out."[2] If you have every answer, what hope do you need? What help? How could you grow in your faith if you knew everything?

I think if you don't have some question of your own, you may actually be very insecure and lacking in your faith. Nineteenth century British evangelist Charles Spurgeon agrees and says, "While men have no faith, they are unconscious of their unbelief; but, as soon as they get a little faith, then they begin to be conscious of the greatness of their unbelief."[3]

Spurgeon understood that unbelief stems from some level of belief. True faith is having good reason for our hope, not knowing all the answers, but knowing enough to act anyways. True faith is comfortable enough to ask questions and confess some unbelief, because the other 99 truths in which you are confident are stronger than the few questions you wrestle with. Your questions, asked within the borders of faith, now lead to knowing and growing even more reasons for hope.

Matthew Lee Anderson explains the difference between doubt and questioning like this:

> Doubt seems to be more of a state or condition, while questioning is a pursuit. When we doubt, we hesitate over whether to welcome or accept what is before us. We waver in our stance and hold ourselves back from committing ourselves. The posture of doubt is even different from outright unbelief: it is neither the boldness of an outright rejection or the humility of belief. It is, instead, a vacillating double-mindedness that prevents us from living a fully integrated life within the world.[4]

Don't mistake questions and doubt. Questioning leads to understanding, growth and trust in the Lord. Questioning is a cry for help, a desire to move from unbelief to belief as we seek affirmation of what we already trust.

Doubting leads to absolutely nothing, except splinters in your bottom from sitting on the fence. It restricts the potential for a more profound faith that could finally empower you to act. It lacks enough courage to walk away and say "no" and lacks conviction enough to say "yes." The only thing doubt produces is an excuse to wait. *Someday* is the fruit of doubt. Instead of trusting Jesus enough to confess our unbelief, we hide behind our unexpressed doubts.

God is not afraid of your doubts or your questions, because He doesn't fear the truth. Let us seek and discover all we can with a childlike, humble heart. Let us repent of our prideful independence and return to an innocent need for understanding from our Father.

Reject the notion that following Jesus means we have it all figured out. Be humble enough to admit you lack understanding. Pursue a depth to your belief that allows you to trust the Gospel enough to come as you are, knowing that since God was willing to give His only son, surely He is glad to give us more faith when we confess we don't trust Jesus enough.

CONFESSING UNBELIEF

Through tear-filled eyes, the father desperately looked up at Jesus. His only hope was that his humble confession of weak belief would be enough for Jesus to help his unbelief. Mark doesn't record how much time elapsed between the father's confession and Jesus' first step of action, but any second of delay must have been agonizing.

Then Jesus relieved the tension with His own sufficiency, resoundingly answering the "If you can" clause of the father's original plea. The story concludes with the child shrieking one final time as he convulsed violently and lay limp in the dirt. The crowd surmised the boy was dead, but Jesus walked over and gently lifted him to his feet. He was truly alive for the first time in years. The child had new life. The father had new faith.

For us to be people who respond to God-sized things that our Savior asks of us, we must get in the habit of confessing all unbelief. The effects of unbelief go far beyond our state of cognitive agreement. As Jeff Vanderstelt states in his book *Gospel Fluency,* "Our behaviors are the tangible expressions of our beliefs."[5] If you want to summarize what you believe, look no further than how you act. Our attempts to respond faithfully will never be sustained without an undergirding deep belief. If we never address our incorrect root belief or confess our state of unbelief, we'll never move the arc of our actions beyond temporary behavior modification.

Vanderstelt goes on to say we shouldn't just repent of our wrong behaviors, but repent of our wrong beliefs. Many of us are aware of active or passive disobedience we have presented to God year after year but we've never taken the time to identify the doubt at the root of that fruit. For us to live a life empowered by the Gospel, we must replace every lie we believe with the truth of who God is. Have enough faith to confess that you don't have enough faith and ask Jesus to help your unbelief.

Maybe you don't believe Jesus provides, so you aren't willing to change jobs or travel to a mission site. At the root of it, you don't trust Him to be enough.

Maybe you have a hard time believing He is best. Comfort, position, savings, sex or people's opinion all seem a little more important than obeying Jesus. At the root of it, you don't see Him as good.

Maybe you don't believe Jesus will impart the wisdom and power you need to step into a new position of leadership in your church, career or community, so you wait. At the root of it, you don't trust Him to be with you.

Maybe a part of you doesn't believe Jesus is real. You've heard the stories and nodded your head, but to be honest, you aren't sure He's worth the sacrifice the Christian life involves, because you aren't sure He's even there for you.

The fact is, you become like that in which you believe. If we don't believe Jesus is enough, we will never become like Him. Jesus himself says in John 14:12: "Very truly I tell you, whoever believes in me will do the works I have been doing, and they will do even greater things than these."

We have the opportunity to do even more than Jesus did! We have the Spirit empowering us and the gospel carrying us. Jesus loves us enough to call and equip us for great things if we believe. We don't have to possess perfect faith to be perfectly accepted and sent. But to step into the higher callings that God has for our lives, we must believe He is enough.

Are you allowing doubts to play on the playground of unexpressed thoughts in your mind? If so, kick them out! Right now, get out a sheet of paper and write down all of the things that you don't believe about Jesus. Then ask Him to help you believe! Confess this unbelief out loud. Have confidence that He is for you and will help you. God is equipping us one confession at a time. When we finally have enough faith to question and confess unbelief, we give ourselves the foundation needed to tackle those *someday* aspirations.

The question is, do you trust Him enough to ask for help?

ASK YOURSELF:

- Do I trust Jesus enough to offer Him my questions?

- Do I truly believe Jesus loves me enough to help me overcome my unbelief?

- What doubts about Jesus do I need to confess to Him so that my faith can grow?

- How have these doubts kept me from taking steps of faith?

PART 2
LOVED ENOUGH

CHAPTER 4
EMPOWERED BY GRACE

SINGING OVER ME

One of my favorite things about being pastor of a young church is getting to watch first-time parents adore their newborn child. Nothing makes a grown man melt like cradling his infant daughter in his arms. His pride and joy radiates across the room. Though they look like they've been hit by a truck due to weeks of stress and lack of sleep, they would declare it is totally worth it. They'd do anything for their child.

God is so good to wire us this way. He made us to be profoundly attached to our children before they are even born! Without that emotional commitment, I don't know how anyone would overcome the challenges of raising a child.

Think about it. A newborn contributes absolutely nothing to the family's well-being. They just offer demanding cries, smelly diapers and projectile vomit. They're a massive hit on your finances and will never pay a bill. At risk of being overly dramatic, newborns are parasites in the family fur. When evaluated superficially, they have nothing to offer, yet they require so much.

Nothing in the world demands love and attention so freely as our children. Yet, we delight in providing for them, sacrificing for them without obligation and no expectations, other than maybe a little giggle when playing peekaboo. We'll find our joy in the simplicity of singing a lullaby as we rock them to sleep. Why? How could we give our lives to someone who does nothing for us? Why do we love someone so much before they even come into the world?

The question seems complicated, but the answer is simple. We have been made in the image of God. God loved us, his children, before we had anything to offer Him. He knew us before we were knit together in our mother's womb (Psalm 139:13). We too reflect this quality because God installed His nature in us. You love your child like you do because that child belongs to you. He or she is yours, and that is enough.

A line I sing over and over in my head is from Cory Asbury's hit song, "Reckless Love." The song starts with a truth that reflects the Father's heart: *"Before I spoke a word, You were singing over me."* Is it possible that before I was even cognizant, before I had the ability to whisper a word of praise, before I gave Him my life and presented my body as a living sacrifice, that God Himself was singing over me? The answer is a resounding yes! The God I sing praises to also sings songs of joy over me.

In Zephaniah 3:17 it says, "The Lord your God is with you, the Mighty Warrior who saves. He will take great delight in you; in his love he will no longer rebuke you, but will rejoice over you with singing."

In a time when God's people had chosen false gods over Him, the Lord made a promise that rings true today. Speaking through the prophet Zephaniah, God pronounces judgment on His people, intending to purify them and bring them back again. At the tail end of this proclamation of retribution, a promise is made. Today this promise is freely offered to all because of our mighty warrior, Jesus.

Because of Jesus' willingness to fight our battle of sin and death, we can not only be saved from rebuke and punishment, but actually become God's delight. If you trust Jesus Christ to be your Lord and

Savior, He not only takes away your sin, He gives you a new title—that of His child. A child in whom He takes great satisfaction. A child that He rejoices over in singing.

Just as a father's delight is not conditional on what his child has to offer, our Heavenly Father delights in us way before we could do anything to please Him. Just as a Father loves his children for no other reason than that they are his, so does God love His children. The fact that God delights over you in singing simply because He chooses to should be the most freeing truth in your life. Because Jesus gladly rescues us at our worst, we are free from trying to earn His delight. He gives it before we ever seek it. Our Heavenly Father indescribably loves His children.

THE TITLE OF DAD

Hall of Fame boxer Ken Norton earned plenty of titles over the course of his life. Before claiming the WBC heavyweight title in 1978, he was most known for breaking Muhammad Ali's jaw when he beat him by split decision in 1973. Norton could easily have considered the worldwide fame of his legendary boxing career as his most significant accomplishment.

Instead, he proudly said in his book, "Going The Distance", "Of all the titles that I've been privileged to have, the title of 'dad' has always been the best."[1] Norton knew that being a dad wasn't an obligation. It was a privilege and he was grateful for it.

I can't help but believe our Heavenly Father feels the same way. Take a moment to think of all the titles our God has rightfully earned. He is the Creator of all things; Redeemer of all that is broken; Almighty Savior; King of Kings; Lord of Lords; Prince of Peace. We will spend all of eternity proclaiming the wonderful attributes and titles of our God, never running out of things to praise because of the vastness of who He is. Among all of these rightful names and lofty titles of our Holy Lord, I can't help but think He would agree with Norton. Of all the titles that God has been privileged to have, the title of 'dad' has always been the best.

For us to be empowered to do great things, we must trust our Heavenly Father is behind us every step of the way. Our Father isn't there because He has to be. God is proud to be your Dad. He is doing what He loves most when He is with you. He loves to provide for His children, to protect, to listen to your problems. He sings over you as you confide in Him.

The Apostle John writes in 1 John 3:1, "See what great love the Father has lavished on us, that we should be called children of God!" And that is what we are! God gave up His own child to call us His children. The love required to redeem us from judgment cost Him everything and He never withholds that great love. He lavishes it over every one of us who come to Him like a child, seeking Jesus to be our "enough." When we do, we are reminded that we are nothing less than a child of the King.

DELIGHT IN GOD'S DELIGHT OF YOU

If you have entrusted your life to Jesus, you have to do nothing else to bring a smile to Our Heavenly Father's face. When He gazes upon you, He sees the perfection of His Son which causes Him to delight in you exactly as you are.

In a time when the world will sell you any title you can imagine, let no one but God tell you who you are. Proclaim that you are who He says you are! You are His joy. He cherishes you enough to sing over you.

You aren't a failure, unredeemable, unloved or unknown. You don't need to do better to be accepted. God's delight in you isn't determined by whether or not you finally have enough knowledge, experience or credentials to do something significant. He isn't prouder to be your Father because you got promoted, or won the game, or even because you are praying more.

Before you had anything to offer, He was singing over you.

He was proud to be your Abba before you cried for your mama. Understanding God's delight in us should embolden us to step out. We have a strong, loving Daddy who will always be there for us!

Confident in that, we can begin to take risks, to step into the unknown. We're motivated to settle for nothing less than our best. Why? Because our strong Daddy supports and loves us, win, lose or draw. We no longer fear failure, because even in failing we know our Father is proud of our efforts. We cannot and will not be shaken. We are empowered by Grace.

How long have we ignored this power?

EMPOWERED. NEVER SPOILED.

Galatians 5:13 talks about the freedom of servitude. It says, "You, my brothers and sisters, were called to be free. But do not use your freedom to indulge the flesh; rather, serve one another humbly in love."

If ever there was a man who knew what it meant to live enslaved, it was Paul. For decades, he roamed his world powerful and free. But not even he realized how he was chained to the weight of religious good works. Years later, after encountering and following Jesus, he was thrown into jail, tied to whipping posts and confined by shackles. Yet, for the first time in his life, Paul was free—free from works, guilt and shame. The grip of sin and death no longer confined Him. Paul was free and ready to use his freedom to accomplish great things.

On a typical Thursday afternoon, as I often do, I went to the Washington County Detention Center to visit my friend Jahmar Adams. That day, I gained a new perspective on freedom. Jahmar had been incarcerated about 6 months before starting to follow Jesus. During that time, I had shared the Gospel with him often, and he was being discipled by an older prisoner named Mr. J. After weeks of hearing about God's grace, Jahmar's life changed forever after receiving the freedom that Jesus offers.

He often reminded me just how free he was. He'd say, "I may be in that cell 23 hours a day, but they can never take my freedom. I am as free as I have ever been. I will be His forever."

Jahmar was freer than many people who come and go from churches today. As he began to experience this freedom for the first time, He taught me a new perspective on unconditional freedom in Christ.

About 10 months into his sentence, as we were catching each other up on our week, I looked at my friend through the thick glass window that separated us and I had a sincere desire to hug him. He had truly become my brother and my heart ached for him to be out. Instead, I had to settle for the cold, hard glass surface as we came as close as we could to bumping fists. Through the outdated, dirty, static rattled telephone that was against my cheek, I asked Jahmar a question. His response shaped my perspective on freedom in a way for which I wasn't ready.

"Man, what is the first thing you're going to do when you get out?" I already had my answer in mind. I would find the nicest meal I could, as quickly as I could. Week after week Jahmar told me how awful the prison food was and I figured a juicy burger or a thick steak would be his focus. Instead, he said without hesitation, "I would for sure go and see my family. I'd then start trying to tell my story to as many young kids as I could. I don't want any of them to end up here. I know what I'm supposed to do in life and it's finding those who are on track to end up here and point them to something better. I want to keep as many people as I can from ending up where I am right now."

Unlike my idea, nothing about Jahmar's answer was self-serving. Jahmar, a brand-new believer, already knew what it meant to use his freedom to serve, much better than me. In fact, he embodied the command in Galatians 5 to "not use your freedom to indulge the flesh; rather, serve one another humbly in love."

Jahmar was empowered by grace. I was spoiled by it.

All who trust Jesus as their Lord and Savior have been smothered in grace. Grace is more complex than I fully understand, but in its simplest form it is a gift freely given, expecting no payment in return. Through Jesus, God has lavished grace on us so thick we can't even begin to understand just how free we are. However, we should seek to understand it more. It has always been God's desire for us to be stewards of His grace. From the air we breathe to the future inheritance we've been promised, awareness of these gifts should make us totally unsatisfied to settle for our own desires. This foundation and freedom in Christ should spur us to action, just like it did for Jahmar. We should allow it to empower us to do more.

THE SPOILED SON

I get pretty frustrated when I think of all of the unsatisfied, spoiled rich kids I've met over the years. You know the kids I'm talking about. Their parents give them everything, yet they appreciate nothing, and seem to waste it all. With all the money, education, support and opportunity lavished on them, they should be doing so much more.

Instead, the blessings that should empower them, actually excuses them. They've been given all they need. Why get a job? Why finish my degree? Why serve others? They frivol away the rocket fuel that should launch them. They are spoiled by grace. And you know what? So am I.

When I slow down enough to remember all I have, I realize my Heavenly Father also has given me all I could ever need—a wonderful wife, fantastic job, unconditional acceptance and hope for the future. But instead of utilizing this grace for greater service and more Kingdom effectiveness, too often I settle, satisfied. Instead of stepping eagerly into the unknown, I coast into the constant, content in comfort. I become a barn for the grace I've been given instead of a vessel that passes it on.

When I think of how God accepts me, of all He has given me, I realize how much more I have to offer. I put off things for *someday* because I am too focused on using my freedom for myself instead of embracing it to step boldly into service and sacrifice. Grace sours quickly when stagnant. Where have you settled for being spoiled by grace, instead of stirring it to pass on to others?

The more I think about how I hoard my Father's love instead of spreading it for something great, the more I identify with the Prodigal Son. The prodigal, in the Bible, is a son who finally learns just how loved he is, a son who receives a second chance he didn't deserve, a son who experienced grace and had to make a choice of what to do with it.

In Luke 15, Jesus tells a powerful parable familiar today even among people who have never cracked open a Bible. A master storyteller, Jesus addresses two types of sinners seated around him. He speaks to those who are far from God because of what they do wrong —prostitutes, tax collectors and others labeled by Luke as "sinners". Jesus also addresses those who are far from God because of what they do right —Pharisees and Scribes, who trust their own works to justify them. Both are far from the Father and Jesus wants them to come back.

The story starts with a wealthy man and two sons. The sons enjoy their father's wealth and know that at his death, they will inherit it as their own. In the meantime, the father supported his family and workers by the income generated from his farm. Because there was no 401k, pension or Social Security, the land was the family's income, retirement plan, security and nest egg to one-day launch the sons with their own families. There was no financial "Plan B." Knowing this, and knowing that he had a substantial future inheritance, the younger of the two sons audaciously makes a request. He asks for his cut of the estate now.

To ask for your inheritance early is insulting today, but was unheard of then. You can almost hear the lips in the audience smacking in disgust as Jesus tells this part of the story. Such a request was to wish your father dead. It was to say, "I don't care about you, I care about your things." The son has settled for the lesser blessing. He would rather claim the possessions of the father than enjoying the position of a son. What happens next is perhaps the most surprising thing in the entire story. Shockingly, the father gives it to him.

The father holds nothing back, sacrificially sells a portion of the property and gives the son his entire share. So much undeserved grace. The son, without even taking time to thank his father, grabs the money and skips town. He travels long and far and does what a spoiled son does best—he wastes it all.

Jesus says the boy, "squandered his wealth in wild living." (v.13) Like a spoiled brat, the son spent all the grace on himself. He wasted his freedom and his father's hard-earned blessing. Instead of being a steward of grace, he squandered it. Soon, he is a pathetic man who is broke, hungry, alone and desperate for grace again, a position far too familiar to many today.

As foolish as this son was, he had enough sense to do one thing right. He knew to return to his father. After being reduced to eating pig food and realizing even his father's servants lived better than him, he swallowed his pride and walked home, no longer seeking grace, but survival. He was now willing to work as a servant for his own dad. Filled with a bit of hope, he comes to his senses and begins his journey home in search of an opportunity to serve the man he betrayed.

As the son approaches home, the father sees him in the distance. Jesus' story implies the father has been waiting for his son's return, and the wait is finally over. The father immediately takes off in a sprint toward his boy. As the son gets closer with every step, he continues to practice his confession and pitch to be hired. Suddenly, he realizes that a man is running towards him. Moments later, much to his surprise, he recognizes that man to be his dad!

Oh no! He hasn't seen his dad move like this in years. An older man of his status and dignity would never move faster than a brisk walk. The son likely thinks his father is furious to run down there and meet him on the road. In a moment, the two men meet, loving father and apprehensive son.

Exhausted, the father approaches his son. He can barely tell it his him, but looking past the dirt, sweat, and matted hair, realizes he once again is looking into the eyes of his boy. Before the son even can start his apology and sales pitch to be hired, the father smothers him with a hug. He kisses the boy between cries of joy! Again, the son tries to open his mouth and express his remorse but the father cuts him off.

"'Quickly!" the father shouts, turning his head back toward the household. "Bring the best robe and put it on him. Put a ring on his finger and sandals on his feet. Bring the fattened calf and kill it. Let's have a feast and celebrate. For this son of mine was dead and is alive again; he was lost and is found." (V.22–24)

That day, the son learned a lesson that must have changed his life forever. He discovered that *who you belong to matters more than what you become.* The father didn't care if his son had become a successful entrepreneur or a street bum. All he cared about was that the boy was in his arms, at home where he belonged.

The son now knew the unconditional acceptance of the father that is needed to free us from ourselves. When you finally realize just how deeply, fully and completely loved you are, despite all of your squandering, you begin to be empowered by grace.

It almost took too long for this prodigal son to learn how loved he was. His selfish ambition kept him from thriving under the acceptance of his own dad. Knowing his father loved him enough to give him a wealthy inheritance while he yet lived should have seeded in him a desire to multiply that grace for something bigger than himself. It should have given him the boldness to risk more knowing that no matter what, he would always have a dad who loves him and is for him. It should have moved him not to abuse this grace but to be empowered by it.

Unfortunately, he saw his blessing as an opportunity for himself alone. Luckily for him, neither his possessions nor his poverty changed his position. Despite his recklessness, nothing could change who he was to his father. Only your father can tell you who you are. When he says you are his child, nothing can change that.

It's a shame we don't hear the rest of this story. We do know it concludes with a massive feast. While people are partying, the self-righteous older brother is pouting over his foolish little brother. Instead of being grateful for his return, he is bitter that the licentious is honored while his own persistent service is ignored. Jesus intentionally left the crowd hanging so we never learn how this family resolved its conflict and started living life together again.

As I think about how the younger brother might respond after the party died down and the sun rose on his restored life, I feel he had a few options.

One option is to walk daily in shame, guilt and embarrassment. He probably looked constantly for ways to pay his father back, to ingratiate himself, to apologize for things already forgiven. For the first time, he might be motivated to work hard for his dad, but this motivation would have been to pay back that which already has been pardoned. The harder he worked, the better he may feel and eventually he may be able to forgive himself, years after his father already had.

The second option is never to take risks again. The last time he did, he messed up big time! He could live a safe life trying not to get in anyone's way. He's already been enough of a burden and a failure, so maybe if he lays low, it will make up for all the past heartache he caused.

He feels guilt and shame as in the previous option, but this response is not to work harder and do more, but to limit his mistakes by doing less. Either way, his motivation is to pay for something he already has freely been offered.

The last option I see reflects the father's desire. The son could be so emboldened by the abundant grace he received, that he does more than his father could ever ask of him. The son realizes how loved he is and that love becomes his motivation. He isn't trying to pay his father back, but merely trying to utilize this second chance to its fullest potential. He knows all his father wants is for him to be his best with no pressure to be perfect. The son realizes that even if he fails, his father, Abba, daddy will never fail him.

Like the prodigal son, I too belong to my Father! And whether or not I become a successful pastor, husband, father, student, coach, bus driver or businessman, I will always know I have a father who claims me, to whom I belong. Because of that, I'm going to go for it!

The father knew that the greatest grace he could give his son wasn't one-third of his estate. The grace most needed was unconditional acceptance. More than any riches, the son needed his father to love him always, fight for him, protect him and accept him. The father was willing to spoil his boy with an early inheritance simply so he could become aware and empowered by a greater grace that had been available the entire time—the grace of belonging to the father.

To be empowered by grace is two dimensional.

First, understand what you have been given and use it to serve one another humbly in love. Your passions, talents, education, experiences and riches are not merely for yourself. We will be spoiled beyond comprehension the day we enter into an eternal inheritance. But for now, we use the daily graces given to us to give God our best.

The second aspect of grace—the more neglected aspect—is simply that belonging to our Heavenly Father is the greatest gift of all. Knowing we don't have to work to be accepted into the family, our labor can be free and full. It is sustained by the joy of belonging, rather than fear of failure.

We've all been given more than we deserve, both a promise of future inheritance and enough grace to get us there. We've all abused those gifts and allowed ourselves to be spoiled. The question is, will you humble yourself, return to a watching Father and let his identity define you? Will you let Him label you His child because of who you are, not what you've become? Have you permitted God's Good News to push you to labor, not *for* a position, but *from* a position?

Take a moment to consider how belonging to Jesus matters more than anything you will ever do. How does that change your motivation to make the most of the grace lavished on you?

The Good News is that only God can tell us who we are. Let that identity change our lives and empower us to bring life change to others.

DEFINED AND DEDICATED

You will die for that which defines you.

Motivation is highly tied to identity. You'll live for things you enjoy, but that which defines you will demand all that you have. This is excellent news if you identify with something worth giving your life for. Some see themselves as an athlete and are driven to work beyond exhaustion day in and day out to acquire elite status.

Others see themselves as a mother or father, and their primary goal is to see their child succeed. If their child begins to fail, they dedicate everything to give their child the best chance to prosper.

Some allow the world to define them. Daily they absorb messages that they are worthless, fat, stupid, ugly, poor, clumsy or useless. They literally give up their lives because they allow these dark, ugly labels to define them and can't live with that self-perception. Suicide rates continue to rise in our country—suicide is the second leading cause of death for ages 10-24[2] —because we don't understand *what* truly should define us. Or maybe better put, because we don't understand *who* truly should define us.

We are all tempted to live just a portion of our lives for Jesus. We enjoy certain aspects of Him, so that is what we are willing to live for. We like the thought of Him answering requests, so we pray. We enjoy picking and choosing which of His promises to hold true in our lives, so we occasionally read His word. Church services can sometimes be a pleasant experience, so periodically we attend. We are comfortable giving up a percentage of our income, so sometimes we tithe.

The result is a life that lives partly for Jesus, but would never be willing to die for Him. I don't want to live that life any longer.

The reason many of us cannot live bold and obedient lives is because we don't claim our primary identity in how God views us.

We assume an identity as spouse, teacher, parent, athlete, artist or businessman over Child of The One True King. We don't step into our identity as an unconditionally accepted son or daughter and allow it to change everything.

Those who find their identity in Jesus not only give all aspects of life to Him but are willing to die for Him, knowing they are secure the entire time! When you think of those martyred in the early church and those enduring persecution across the world today, they live so securely knowing how God sees them, that they count giving their life for Him as a privilege!

If I can be honest, it is easy for me to say I'm willing to die for Jesus. But when I examine my life, I'm not even able to say I live entirely for Him. I'm not willing to try and fail. I'm not prepared to endure seasons of uncertainty as I give God my "yes" before I am fully qualified. I'm not ready to trust His grace to be sufficient in my weaknesses and shortcomings.

For us to live the fullest life possible for Jesus, we must first be willing to die for Him, and to die to ourselves. We will die for that which defines us. What are you allowing to define you? Is that different than what Jesus says about you? What identity do you need to reject so you can rest in your identity in Christ?

This is the first and most crucial step of allowing grace to empower us to do more. If we believe we belong to Him, we will become what He desires us to be. God's unconditional acceptance gives us permission to "fail." It provides us with confidence to give it our best and not worry about falling short. Whether we overachieve or come up short, we find our comfort and joy in the Person to whom we belong. By the world's standard, we may seem underqualified. By God's standard we always have more than enough because God's grace is sufficient and He has called us His own. With that confidence we can serve one another humbly in love. If we do this, we cannot fail.

We are forever His. Because of that, as we are about to discover in the next chapter, we are now free to swing for the fences.

ASK YOURSELF:

- How has grace changed my life? Has it moved me to do more than I ever thought or imagined I could? Or has it become something I hoard?

- Take a moment now to reflect on all the beautiful gifts God has given. Have I allowed myself to become spoiled by grace, letting grace stagnate in me?

- How could I begin to use the grace given to me by God for something bigger than myself?

- Who or what do I allow to define me?

- How do I need to get back to finding my identity in how God views me because of the grace He gave me through Jesus?

CHAPTER 5
STRIKEOUT SWINGING

SWING BATTER BATTER

Many words describe my wonderful mom. Athlete is not one of them. She is gentle, selfless, kind, beautiful and God-honoring, but she will be the first to tell you that she and the gym are no longer well acquainted. Ironically, she is the only one in our immediate family who played on a college sports team.

Years ago, mom had a pretty successful softball career for a small college in California. Thankfully, she's nothing like *Napoleon Dynamite's* Uncle Rico, who chimes in about the "glory days" every time someone remotely brings up the sport. However, she has told me numerous times how playing softball helped her become pretty good at picking weeds.

Mom wasn't a big fan of her coach, and for good reason. Of the coach's many questionable tactics, the worst may have been her punishment for "striking out looking." Any time a player watched a third strike zip by without swinging at the pitch, that player had to pick weeds in the infield the next day.

The coach wanted players to choke up on the bat and get more aggressive when they had two strikes on them. Few things, if any, frustrate a coach more than a batter watching their final strike cross the plate without swinging at it. I promise you, if I had two strikes on me, I'd swing away at anything close enough to reach. Whether I got out or not, you weren't going to catch me picking weeds in the southern California sun.

Monica Abbott, former University of Tennessee-Knoxville softball pitcher and Olympic silver medalist, consistently threw a softball underhand over 70 mph. She's even reached an unheard of 77 mph![1] That means a batter has less than four-tenths of a second before the ball travels 43 feet from the pitcher's hand to the plate to decide whether to pass or swing. Considering that, maybe it's no wonder so many players strike out looking. If you don't react immediately and instinctively, the opportunity will completely pass you by.

Every day I make hundreds of decisions. Shut off the alarm or hit snooze? Burger or salad? Find my wife for a goodbye kiss, or shout "I love you" as I walk out the door? Long sleeved shirt, or short? Spend a moment in prayer, or scroll through Instagram?

Some days, I have more significant choices to make. Periodically I find myself at a crossroad with a God-sized commitment before me. Should I change majors and pursue full-time ministry or continue to pursue medical school? Do I spend my winter break in Uganda or stay home for the holidays? Do I purchase the large house or the one more in my budget? Every decision is an opportunity—each offers success and failure—and in these moments I must decide quickly to either swing hard or let it pass.

Every indecision is a decision. It may seem like I have time to contemplate my choices, but waiting isn't an option. Every moment I wait, I am making an active decision to let it go. Like a fastball from Monica Abbot, if you hesitate, the opportunity already has passed.

I hate to think how often I spent so much time considering whether an opportunity was worth swinging at, that it passed me altogether. Most decisions are easy to make. It's easy to figure out which pitches are headed towards the dirt. We're smart to let those pass. Once in a while we even get a fat, slow pitch right down the pipe. I'll instinctively swing hard at those pitches, and I usually crush them! It doesn't take an extraordinary athlete to knock those out of the park.

But what about the majority of pitches that just nick the corners of the strike zone? Hittable balls that come so fast, with so much movement, that you let them pass, rather than risk whiffing. Hey, it was likely a bad pitch, right? There's a better one coming. As you decide to let it pass and the ball thuds into the leather mitt behind you, you exhale and enjoy your right decision. You've saved yourself the embarrassment of swinging and missing.

But, then you hear it. The searing umpire's call of "Steeriiikke three!" He belts it out with so much passion it's like he had been waiting for that moment his entire life. That fleeting satisfaction you felt a moment ago? Gone along with the plans you had to enjoy the rest of your day. Now you drag your bat back to the dugout and get ready for an exciting afternoon of picking weeds.

God will only throw so many strikes your way before you are out. You eventually—and quickly—must decide to start that nonprofit organization or go back to school. Opportunities to travel overseas or step into a leadership position at your church won't always be on the table. Chances to invite your neighbor over for dinner or to foster a child should be decided now. God may not make you pick weeds after the game, but if you never swing, you will always miss out on the chance to hit a gamer winner.

Once you are His child, you always will be His child in whom He delights, but if we never swing for fear of missing we could very easily miss out on the experience of contributing to a winning team. When we refuse to swing at imperfect pitches, it reveals we doubt our abilities, our opportunities and ultimately our God. Paralysis sets in and indecision becomes the norm. We continue to hide behind the excuse of waiting *someday* for a "better opportunity." What we fail to realize is that every indecision is a vote to forfeit our right to play.

Let me be clear. I am not saying you should swing at every pitch or that swinging guarantees a home run. Stepping into an upward calling when you sense you are underqualified comes with a lot of uncertainty. Sometimes that mission trip is filled with unforeseen challenges that leave you frustrated and unsure. Maybe that new job comes with a lousy boss who doesn't give you opportunities like she promised. Maybe going back to school hits a wall because your money runs out.

You are not guaranteed to hit it out of the park every time you swing, but at least give yourself a chance. Imagine if you only connected on one fourth of the pitches you decided to swing at hard. Would you look a bit foolish at times? Yes. Would you waste some energy and effort? For sure. Might you even strike out from time to time? Yep. But someone who hits bombs every four pitches will not only guarantee herself a spot on the team but will go down as a legend!

I can't help but think that at the end of our lives we will be remembered for the moments we swung hard and saw God do unexplainable things. Successes from our willingness to swing will dump the memory of any failed attempts into the dust bin of history.

Home runs make the strikeouts worth it. When we settle for just making the team we miss the thrill of making a difference in the game.

STAYING IN THE GAME

I played three years of varsity basketball at a pretty prestigious program. Science Hill High School built a winning tradition and the three years I played were no exception. Our team was filled with Division 1 and 2 athletes who were a lot more talented and athletic than me. I lacked skill and size but my work ethic and basketball IQ carved me a place on the team.

At the time, I was just thrilled to be on such an impressive team. We won tournament after tournament, including an all-expense paid trip to Hawaii. By the end of my senior year, we hadn't lost a regular season conference game in three years and were headed to the Tennessee State semi-finals.

Along this journey, I knew my job as a role player. I was to go in a few minutes each half so the starters could rest. I was one of the few players who really enjoyed setting solid screens, taking charges, protecting the ball and setting up other players to score. I contributed enough to play a few minutes in each game, but I never developed a more significant role.

My biggest regret was not shooting the ball more. I worked on my shot as much as anyone in the offseason and practiced as hard as I could. My shooting percentage was average and would have improved with more in-game reps. My problem was I was afraid to miss. Despite how hard I worked to prepare for the game, I wasn't confident enough to step up and shoot once we were playing in front of a couple thousand people.

My goal was to not mess up. Don't turn the ball over. Don't miss any shots. Don't give the coach a reason to take me out. And that's what I did! I was the best at limiting mistakes. The irony is, the "don't mess up" mindset I thought kept me in the game ultimately brought me back to the bench. Because I was never as valuable as those who confidently tried to put the ball in the basket, I never got to stay in the game.

I wish I had shot more not so I could look back and boast. I should have shot more so I could have contributed more to the team, and so I could have experienced the thrill of both missing and scoring. I should have played more minutes in the game instead of sitting on the sidelines. I thought I was helping by limiting my mistakes, but really, I was hurting the team by never fully utilizing my abilities.

Like basketball, during high school I thought God was asking me simply not to mess up what He was doing in my life. I looked around and knew God was at work so if I could just not mess anything up by getting drunk, having sex, trying drugs or talking too foolishly, I could be on His team. I minimized mistakes and focused on not committing any of the "big" sins, meanwhile wasting years of opportunity, never pushing myself to take shots at God-given moments to excel.

I have been haunted for years by the question, "If you don't, who will?" I'm not sure where I first heard it, but it has influenced my life beyond any other question that has crossed my mind. Think about it. If you don't share Jesus with your neighbor, who will? If you don't invite that family into your home to live with you during a difficult season of their life, who will? If you don't become the best teacher you can become to help students love to learn, who will? If you don't plant a church, become a friend, write a book, coach a team, set an example of living a pure life, who will?

When I played basketball, I assumed someone else was going to score. We had plenty of great players, I just had to get out of their way and set them up to succeed. And yes, my mistakes were minimal, but so were my contributions. At what expense was I passing up an easy shot to get the ball to someone else to take a more difficult one? I never took that "If you don't, who will?" mindset into the game. I just assumed I was a role player, not qualified to be more. At least, not yet I wasn't. Maybe I wasted an opportunity to progress as a player because I didn't trust that I'd ever get there. Unfortunately, I settled for where I was and never risked enough to develop where I could be.

I never developed my fullest potential as an athlete because I wasn't willing to risk a miss. Yet, it is from our misses that we learn the most. It is from our previous failures that we develop the courage to miss again. Eventually, we realize our misses don't have the dire consequences we feared. Besides, the more I shoot and miss, the more I can correct my shot. It gives my coach a chance to speak into me and develop me for something better next game.

A coach can best work with a player who is willing both to take the shot and be corrected. Jesus is the same! If we are eager to shoot and happen to miss He will instruct and develop us for next time.

We will come out even more qualified in the long term because we erred on the side of action. Jesus helps us learn as we go! Even misses become a blessing that assures future growth.

When others try to tell us we are too inexperienced, too young or too underqualified to take the shot, God tells us something different. He reminds us that He uniquely has chosen us. He asks us, "If you don't, who will?" On God's team, you are the starter. He isn't looking for someone else to come in and replace you. He isn't going to bench you for your first mistake. God's reckless love for you should give you the confidence to be a little reckless yourself. His trust in you should give you a swagger that is greater than the fear of missing.

You know you are getting better with every shot you take, so look to shoot as often as you can. Efficiency comes in second to initiative because efficiency improves on the other side of action. Missed shots and risky passes are a part of getting buckets and diming out assists. It may be too late for me to develop into an outstanding athlete, but God isn't done coaching me. He continues to mature me through experience.

Maybe you are underqualified. Perhaps you aren't prepared yet. But understand that you'll never do more until you refuse to play scared. So, get to shooting.

COMMIT. DON'T OMIT.

In Romans chapter 5, the Apostle Paul lays out how eternal life comes through the life-changing grace that only Jesus can offer. He finishes the chapter by explicitly explaining, "So that, just as sin reigned in death, so also grace might reign through righteousness to bring eternal life through Jesus Christ our Lord." (v.21) You don't need a seminary degree to understand how much you need God's grace. All you really need is the first five chapters of Romans to begin to understand how the precious grace that cost Jesus everything is freely offered to us.

Paul, being a smart guy, looked ahead to how this Good News too easily could become cheap grace. God's people have a history of mismanaging His blessings. Chapter 6 starts with Paul asking and answering his own question. "What shall we say, then? Shall we go on sinning so that grace may increase? By no means! We are those who have died to sin; how can we live in it any longer?" (v.1–2)

Growing up, I understood this scripture as a way to discourage me from doing wrong. Don't drink, smoke, cuss, or have sex before marriage. Even though God's grace can cover the sins of a repentant heart, we're not to go on sinning. Cheating on a test or lying to a loved one becomes easier if you know you'll be forgiven, but that cheap view of grace will never free you from a life of sin. I am thankful for this verse because it helps motivate me to abstain from things that would be harmful to my health and detrimental to my sanctification.

My problem early in my Christian walk was that I understood only half of this command. I thought about it only in terms of what I shouldn't be doing, instead of what God has freed me to do.

Too often we misuse grace as a pass to continue doing all the wrong things we know we shouldn't. These sins of actively choosing to do wrong are called sins of commission. They should occur less and less as we allow God's Spirit to make us more into His image. So yes, we should stop lying and lusting. We should not covet or curse.

Most Christ followers don't have a problem focusing on quitting these sin habits. In fact, they can assume a lot of false pride when they give up an addiction or bad practice. As important as it is to repent of these actions, at what expense are we overly focused on them? Could our obsession with never doing wrong be causing us to neglect the other, more important half of our purpose?

To live fully in the freedom that grace purchased for us, we must also repent of all we have neglected to do. So many commands in God's word are not commands to stop, but to start! Feed the hungry. Care for the orphan. Love your neighbor. Visit the widow. Give thanks. Build one another up. Reprove openly. Be a peacemaker.

The second half of rejecting sin and responding to grace means acting on the commands to love and serve.

Jesus' brother defines the negligent aspect of sin in James 1:7 as, "If anyone, then, knows the good they ought to do and doesn't do it, it is sin for them." Sin is not limited to the acts of disobedience we commit, but includes the acts of obedience we omit!

We rarely focus on these sins of omission, settling instead for simply not messing up. Jesus wants more than that! He wants you to become more like Him, worrying less about doing wrong and focusing more on doing the work of the Father.

The surest way to become more like Jesus is to repent of sins of omission as much as you do sins of commission. When we ignore the sins of "not doing," we pass on the opportunity to live like Jesus and to be fully utilized by the Father.

WILLING TO FIGHT

George B. McClellan possessed all the qualifications and experience to make a great general. A straitlaced and clean-cut war veteran, he graduated second in his West Point class of 1842. From there, he served under General Winfield Scott in the Mexican War.[2] His resume said he was ready to step into one of the most critical leadership positions our country had ever known. President Abraham Lincoln picked him to lead the Union army in the American Civil War.

You may be thinking, if this man was such an essential part of our country's history, why have I never heard of him? It's because he didn't keep this position long enough to be regularly remembered 150 years later. McClellan played it too safe.

As good as he was at preparing for battle, McClellan was deficient in executing once the fighting started. Known for having "analysis paralysis" McClellan's reluctance to take action and bring the fight to the Confederacy ultimately got him replaced just a year later by a man whose name you do recognize. Lincoln needed someone who was ready to fight, a leader not afraid to initiate and execute on the battlefield. Someone whose *someday* was today. Lincoln found that man in Ulysses S. Grant.

Although Grant was available when Lincoln picked McClellan, a quick glance will tell you why he wasn't Lincoln's first pick. Grant finished in the lower half of his West Point class. He had a reputation for drinking heavily and smoking like a train. Grant was impulsive on a good day and reckless on a bad one. He was highly criticized—and rightfully so—for the number of casualties he was willing to endure to secure a victory. As a result, people often called for his job. When Lincoln was confronted with pressure to dismiss Grant, he responded with, "I can't spare this man, he fights."[3]

As far as Lincoln was concerned, Grant knew how to fight. More importantly, Grant knew how to win. Very quickly, Grant began to rack up victories in the deep south. Where McClellan struggled to engage the enemy, Grant excelled in it. Eventually, Grant took over for McClellan and secured victory for the Union army, only a year after being appointed General-in-Chief.

Not every move that Grant made was ethical or could be considered a picture perfect example of leadership. However, I think he is a prime example of how a willing spirit can make up for an inadequate resume.

Many of us can identify with Grant. We've never excelled at anything. We have a bit of a dark past. Maybe we have a history of making the wrong decision and taking heat for it. Know, however, that even in such a state we have incredible potential. God will use you to accomplish amazing things if you simply are willing to fight. More than anything, Jesus wants a fighter on His team.

I am humbled when I think about how our heavenly Father trusts us to "fight the good fight of faith" (1 Timothy 6:12) and to be "a good foot soldier of Christ Jesus" (2 Timothy 2:3). We have a battle ahead that is worth fighting, and luckily, we are not waging this war alone. We have a leader who guides us every step of the way and always makes the right call. He is a general who fights our battles for us and with us. He is Jesus, and He invites us to join the action.

God has appointed some of you as sergeants as you actively oversee and command many. Others, for now, are to be faithful foot soldiers, following your leader into battle. Wherever you find yourself, one thing is certain. The surest way never to see victory is refuse to join the battle. Strategy, training, experience and credentials mean nothing if you aren't willing to take that final step into the fight.

I think the Lord would rather have 300 good privates eager to fight than 3,000 generals looking only to plan. As we trust our King to equip us, we anticipate the visceral rush of enjoining the battle with Him.

When you take a moment to reflect on the fact that you are loved enough to die for, it should shape you into a "yes man" or a "yes woman." When you begin really to trust that *belonging* matters more than *becoming*, you will operate in the confidence of your identity as a child of the King. You know that even if you swing and miss, you still come back to a Father who loves, accepts and shapes you, even in your shortcomings. He is proud of your efforts and will equip you for future success through your previous failures.

What are you hesitating about that God is inviting you to step into wholeheartedly? Into what battle is He asking you to charge? You are loved enough to do it. The pitch is coming. Swing batter batter.

ASK YOURSELF:

- *"If you don't, who will?"* How does this question change my thoughts toward the actions I am tempted to put off for another day?

- What have I deferred that God is asking me uniquely to step into?

- Do I think about sins of omission as much as sins of commission?

- What sins of omission do I need to turn from and begin giving God my "yes" as an act of worship to Him?

- How has analysis paralysis limited my availability to accomplish God-sized acts in my life?

PART 3
YOUNG ENOUGH

CHAPTER 6
WHAT A TIME TO BE ALIVE

ASKING THE RIGHT QUESTION

Where will I be in five years?

You've probably thought about that question a lot. I know I have. Especially if you're young, establishing a family, a career, being mobile, it's impossible not to think about it. Over the past five years I've been bombarded continuously by friends and family curious about where I planned to live, what job I wanted, who I will marry, and now, when I will have children. Naturally I look ahead and try to gain some clarity for myself to these questions.

It's fun to think about the future. It's also wise and responsible. However, as important as it is to work toward something not yet attained, I think "Where do you want to be in five years?" isn't the best question to focus on. It's shallow, limited and temporary. It subconsciously gives you permission to focus on the future at the expense of the present. It assumes you have five years to live and casts the destination as more important than the journey.

Let's consider a better question, an inquiry that ultimately will get us home without neglecting the intentionality needed to get there. This question must hold influence over anything else that fights for our focus. It's a question that a close friend of mine took seriously and because of that, hundreds of lives were changed for eternity.

The question is this: *Over the next five years, how do I want my life to impact eternity?* Your answer changes everything.

My friend Gavin Duncan graduated from Science Hill High School at the top of his class in the spring of 2010. His senior year he was captain of the basketball team, his face and winsome personality known to everyone. He was my point guard and my good friend. I looked up to him, mostly because of his work ethic and humility. It was admirable and contagious.

In August 2010, Gavin entered the University of Tennessee-Knoxville to study engineering, focused on working hard to get to where he wanted to be in five years.

Two years later I started at UT-Knox and ran into Gavin. Immediately I realized something had changed. Gavin was always an admirable guy, but now the love and grace of Jesus had changed his life and he lived to share it. The way he sacrificially cared for others and loved Jesus with all of his heart was different than anything I had experienced. It was real. It was infectious. I wanted it.

Gavin began to mentor me and lead our freshman Bible study. But more than just teaching students, he lived life with us, always modeling what it looked like to be a servant leader. I couldn't help but notice how he worked hard but still made time for others. I noted his patience and wisdom. He shared Jesus with others in a way that was relatable and bold. I wanted to be just like him.

For the next two years, Gavin invested deeply in a group of about ten young men. None of us were the same by the end of it. Each of us grew into men of God who are now seeking to do more than we could have imagined just five years ago.

In August 2014, my junior year had just started. Gavin graduated with a degree in civil engineering and began an internship with CRU, the campus ministry in which we were both involved. We had a dream and plan to do incredible things on our campus that year.

I was leading a freshman Bible study, just as Gavin had done two years earlier, and he was going to coach and guide me every step of the way. I was totally confident in the life change we were about to experience and help bring to others. And then I got the phone call.

"Gavin's at UT-Med," my friend, Sam, said. "He's been in a bad accident. You need to get here ASAP." I could tell by Sam's tone it was serious. I gathered my roommates, and we hurried to the hospital.

I spent most of that day and night in the waiting room with my friends and a couple dozen others. I prayed harder than I ever had, crying out to God to save my friend, my mentor, my hero. At 5:30 a.m. the next morning, I learned Gavin wasn't going to make it. Naturally I screamed out in anger to God. I couldn't grasp that this was really happening. Finally, my friends and I went home to rest for a few hours. We knew we'd need it for the long and emotional day ahead.

A few hours later, I went back to visit Gavin one final time. I held his hand and told him I loved Him. I thanked him for all he had done. Four years later, I still can't fully grasp his impact on my life. It seemed so insufficient to sum up all he had done for me in just two plain words of "thank you." But those were the only words I could muster at that moment. I told him to give Jesus a big hug for me and I said goodbye to my best friend before he went to be with Jesus and hear the sweet words, "Well done good and faithful servant."

As I consider Gavin's legacy, I thank God that Gavin's focus wasn't merely on his destination. He didn't devote his attention to reach age 25, be married and wealthy. Gavin's destination took back seat to the process of impacting as many lives as he could for eternity on the journey. His future destination simply came at the end of wherever God took him daily to make a difference. Gavin opened his life to let Jesus use him any way that impacted lives eternally. I thank God he did because without Gavin's pursuit of me to become a servant leader, I wouldn't be writing this book today.

Gavin took that question of, "Over the next five years, how do you want your life to impact eternity?" seriously. He knew life was too short and his purpose was too great for him only to focus on himself. We must focus not just on where we want to be, but more importantly, on who we want to impact along the way.

Our lives will not go as planned. If you define success as reaching your destination instead of by how you lived to get there, you will be judging your life all wrong. Over the next five years, you will encounter unexpected illness, job loss, busted relationships, and even the death of loved ones or yourself. Your only guarantee is that at some point, something unexpected will happen.

However, if we focus on investing for eternal results in the lives of people, no matter where we find ourselves in five years—or at the end—our lives will have been well lived. This mindset is the one constant that will always point us back to true north, no matter where we find ourselves in life.

I thank God that even though Gavin's life didn't go as planned, dying at 23 years old, it was full and fruitful, because he lived his last four years with an eternal perspective.

WATTBA

It is when you shift your focus from destination to process, that the perfect time to be alive becomes now. Or as Grammy award-winning hip-hop artist, Aubrey Drake Graham simply put it, "What a time to be alive!"[1] There is no better time to impact lives eternally around you than now.

Whether you are 13, 33, or 83 years old, you need not wait until you arrive at your desired destination to start living each day to its fullest. The lives around you will not wait. Their needs cannot be put on hold until you feel comfortable and ready. Realize it or not, you were made for moments like the ones you are living right now.

When you read the book of Esther, you clearly see how much influence one person's actions can have. If I may, I'd like to sum up a powerful story of how God uses bold decisions to change lives.

One hundred years after the Babylonian exile, many Jews still had not returned to Jerusalem. Instead, they had settled in the Persian capital of Susa. During this time, the Persian king sought a new queen and in a completely unforeseeable turn of events, he chose Esther, a young Jewish woman.

The king did not know Esther was a Jew, and she didn't tell him as she started her new life of royalty. As nice as this sounds, it didn't take long for Esther to be thrown a curveball. Not long after she came to the king's court, Persian leaders who did not like the foreign immigrants living among them pushed through a decree that within 11 months, all Jews in the city will be annihilated.

Quickly, Mordecai, one of Esther's older Jewish relatives, insists she do something. He tells her to advocate for her people and plead to the king for mercy. Hey, why not? She's his wife, his queen, right? Surely Esther could initiate a simple conversation to save her people.

The only problem is, if anyone approaches the king without being summoned by the king, that person is subject to death. Naturally, Esther reminds Mordecai of why she's probably not the one to influence the King. She is only a young woman, operating under a false identity, and is a member of the very tribe the king says he will eradicate.

At this moment, Esther has a decision to make—risk her life to save many, or hide behind the fact that she isn't qualified to initiate a conversation with the king. Into this dilemma, Mordecai speaks truth.

> Mordecai sent this reply to Esther: "Don't think for a moment that because you're in the palace you will escape when all other Jews are killed. If you keep quiet at a time like this, deliverance and relief for the Jews will arise from some other place, but you and your relatives will die. Who knows if perhaps you were made queen for just such a time as this?" (Esther 4:13–14 NLT)

Mordecai's confidence is not in Esther, but in the Lord. He knows God will be faithful. He also knows that if Esther decides to do nothing, she is choosing to do something. She is choosing to neglect the opportunity—at some risk to herself—to save thousands of others. She can't hide from the present reality by focusing on a future possibility. The future depended on her actions now. She was made for such a time as this.

All of us have these Esther 4:14 moments. For some, they come when we are older. Others are in the midst of their moment as they read this page. When we limit our actions as suitable only to a certain age or qualification we miss out on being a key part in these moments—moments that impact both your life and the lives around you.

Esther ultimately responded to her moment by listening to Mordecai. She bravely approached the king, revealed her true identity, persuaded him to cancel the decree and helped her family and the Jews prosper for years to come. What a time it was to be alive! Esther risked her life, saved thousands of others and experienced God at work in the process. And to think, she almost talked herself out of it.

I WOULD, BUT...

We're all experts at coming up with excuses that let us rock on our *someday* porch while watching the action comfortably from a distance. We tell ourselves we are willing to respond to God's prodding, yet quickly proceed to insert our favorite rationalization when opportunities arise. *"I would, but..."*

We point to other people more apt for the job and then defer to them. We name all the difficulties that would come with a commitment, and declare we're not yet ready to handle them. We like to hide behind the excuse of uncertainty and wait for further revelation to be sure this is really "in God's will."

One common excuse, accepted by others who like to offer the same justification, is that we just don't have enough time. We're certain our next season of life will be "less busy" and then we comfortably start rocking on the *someday* porch, knowing deep down nothing will change. Think about the last time your life was "less busy." As soon as we take one thing off our plates, one or three more unexpectedly jumps on. Life changes. Nothing stays the same. But one thing is certain. An obedient life is never less busy.

Another favorite excuse that we let hamstring our resolve is to feel we are too young for the challenge. No matter your age, you always think you'll be better prepared for it in a few more years. The pressure to acquire another degree, a few more years of savings, or another half decade of "life experience" tempts us enough to trust our future self over the present goodness of the God who calls us higher.

All we hear about is how much we don't know or how little experience we have, instead of trusting how much we would gain after that initial step. We forget how God equips us as we go. Instead of standing apart from the world around us, we follow the path of least resistance. Before we know it, that opportunity we waited on until we were "old enough" is no longer an option. We let others tell us we were too young, a label God never slapped on us.

The greatest qualification that God requires is a pure and contrite heart that seeks after Him. God can change the world with that! Our age, experience, expertise and free time all fall second to the priority of a willing spirit that seeks after God's desires.

For a real-life example, look at the life of David in the books of 1 and 2 Samuel. David was too young, too small and too inexperienced to slay a giant and lead a nation. At least that's what others told him.

David didn't let such labels limit him. His focus was on whatever God wanted him to do, because he trusted God to enable him. He knew the right time to serve God was in the present, so he refused to wait. This attitude and willingness ultimately landed him on the throne and he led God's people into prosperity for decades.

Saul, the king who David succeeded, was much older, more

accomplished and physically blessed. But Saul did not possess the most important qualification. He lacked a heart for the Lord.

David, a man after God's own heart, not only impacted people while he lived; his actions carried implications far beyond his lifetime. In Acts 13, Paul reflects on how the Savior of the world was birthed out of Israel and he credits David for playing a huge role in that!

> After removing Saul, he made David their king. God testified concerning him: 'I have found David son of Jesse, a man after my own heart; he will do everything I want him to do.' From this man's descendants God has brought to Israel the Savior Jesus, as he promised. (Acts 13:22-23)

So, not only did David's heart for God lead to dramatic life change for him and a nation, but it eventually played a role in bringing salvation to the world hundreds of years later! God wants to use you now to help make the world aware of the salvation at hand. If He can use a young shepherd boy to slay a giant, He can use you in ways beyond your imagination. We just have to be willing to do whatever He asks.

YOUNG ENOUGH TO LEAD

Our world needs more young leaders who love Jesus. We need men and women who lead in their church, lead in their family, lead at their company, lead in their community. We need leaders who will make an impact from their titled positions of authority. We also need people who lead subtly and humbly, affecting others deeply, despite not having a gold-plated sign on their office door. In one sense, true leadership is simple. Not everyone will lead, however, because leadership demands sacrifice.

John Maxwell condenses true leadership to this: "Leadership is influence. Nothing more and nothing less."[2]

Let the simplicity of that definition sink in. If leadership is influence, none of us are too young to lead. Each of us has opportunity to influence others. So, who are you influencing? Even more important, how are you influencing them?

All of us have the potential to lead. Some have responded to leadership opportunities well and lives are being changed. Others are waiting because they don't understand how much influence they could have. Ultimately, at the end of your life, it won't be your resume of accomplishments that people remember. It will be the lifetime of God honoring influence you had on others. Which are you working towards?

LEAVING A LEGACY

If you are at all familiar with the late evangelist Billy Graham, then you know he lived a very accomplished life. He preached to hundreds of millions of people. He wrote over two dozen books that have helped change millions of lives. He counseled a dozen U.S. presidents.[3] After decades of labor and humble service, Graham was known as America's Pastor. Until the day he died, Feb. 21, 2018, he sacrificially served our world in a way that I admire and desire to imitate.

At the time of Graham's death, testimonies of his influence appeared everywhere. From Twitter to television, the country couldn't stop talking about him. His nationally televised funeral was packed with thousands who both mourned appropriately and celebrated triumphantly. Graham arguably had more impact on more people than any other person across multiple generations. But how?

Others have accumulated similar accomplishments. Plenty of people have spoken before large crowds, written books, counseled presidents and started foundations. Why did Graham's life have so much impact?

Graham's legacy isn't a resume of titles, honors and achievements.

Graham's is a legacy of influence. He is remembered not for all he did, but for the lives he helped to change. His funeral celebrated that legacy. Graham lived for his eulogy. He died with a legacy.

We're tempted to work toward stacking our resume, especially when young. We think if we can just put our heads down and grind, we'll be in position to do something meaningful later. So we focus entirely on getting a degree, work experience, pay raise, promotion.

The problem is, *a position will never matter more than a person.* You will never bring meaningful change if you don't influence people, even if you have the experience and training that says otherwise. Who cares if you've earned a degree, a promotion, or a mortgage? If those things don't influence someone toward a God-saturated life, they're pointless. Never diminish the power of influence. It's all that matters when living toward your eulogy.

Do you sacrifice opportunities to exercise influence to devote time to stack your resume? Are you selling out for a destination and neglecting the journey? Don't wait another day to prioritize influence. We must start to build our legacy when we're young.

Early in life we can begin to make disciples. It is in our youth that we start a movement to care for widows and orphans. It is in our youth that we love foster children, our neighbors, our fellow students and our coworkers. It is in our youth we travel across the world to share the hope of Jesus that knows no boundaries. Why should we wait when we can lead now!

Are you working on your resume or toward your eulogy? Answer that question honestly and make changes accordingly. Only those whose influence reaches beyond themselves leave a positive legacy. Legacies are built on the foundations you started to lay at a young age. Legacies can't be measured because their impact never ends. Resumes will be lost and forgotten. Legacies continue forever. To which are you devoting your life?

A few days after Gavin died, I walked up to the pulpit at his funeral and smiled through tear-filled eyes toward a sanctuary packed with standing room only. More than 500 people Gavin had influenced came to remember him that day. Because of that, it was only appropriate for me to remind them of Gavin's faithfulness, not to himself, but to the Lord.

In those brief seven minutes I had to speak, I didn't dare focus on his accomplishments as an all-conference high school point guard or his 33 ACT score. I didn't even think about mentioning his degree in civil engineering or his college GPA. No one cared about his work experience or the money in his bank account. Today, all those things were irrelevant. The only thing that mattered was that Gavin loved God and Gavin loved people.

So that's what I talked about. I reminded people of how much Gavin lived to love. I preached my guts out on how Jesus changed Gavin's life and how He can change anyone's life. I praised Jesus for the changed life He had brought me and hundreds of others because Gavin lived with a purpose beyond himself. I reminded everyone that Gavin's legacy will live on through the young men to whom he modeled what it meant to be a man of God. I rejoiced that his impact will continue through the friends with whom he shared the hope of Jesus. I exclaimed how the influence he had on each of us will last for generations.

On his journey, Gavin was so consumed with impacting lives that he reached precisely the destination each of us should desire: to know at the end that you left a legacy of influence, to have your eulogy preached by a young man you loved so well, before hundreds of others who testify that your example helped direct them toward God.

And in some cases, perhaps a young man you nurtured will write a book through tear-filled eyes in which he will share how thankful he is to have called you his friend, leader and hero. I am that young man. Gavin Duncan is that hero. His legacy will live forever through his influence on me.

NOTHING ELSE MATTERS

Life is short. God is big. No one is promised another day.

"Our God is able to do immeasurably more than all we ask or imagine, according to his power that is at work within us." (Ephesians 3:20) These facts should inspire us to wait no longer to influence as many lives as we can. Leadership is never age restricted and its impact will grow exponentially. When we invest early into as many lives as we can, we later get to reflect on all we influenced.

At the end of our life, we will look back and realize that only two things mattered: loving God and loving people.

NOTHING ELSE MATTERS.

These are the only two things that will go on forever, so why invest in anything else? If our temporal gains aren't invested in eternal pursuits, we should be pitied. If we have chased accomplishments that will evaporate like morning mist instead of a legacy that honors God and serves His people, we should be ashamed. No matter where you are now, the good news is, it is never too late to begin loving God and loving people.

As I was preparing to plant a church at age 22, a lot of people told me I was too young. They said I needed first to attend seminary. I needed more formal ministry experience. I needed to wait a few years to be sure this was what I wanted. I needed to get married.

After learning I wasn't going to seminary, one lady told my father that she "only lets a trained butcher handle her meat and something as important as ministry should be handled by someone with an adequate education." Such comments hurt me deeply, and at first, discouraged me. These critics had no idea how many hours of prayer and hard work I had invested. They didn't know my heart. They didn't understand my willingness to do whatever asked of me to see this God-sized dream come true.

At the end of the day, I decided there was no better time for this church to be planted than now, and no better place than in Gray, TN. My discouragement morphed into motivation to show how

God can do so much with so little. Because I knew I was made for such a time as this, in 2016 I took my Food Science and Technology degree from the University of Tennessee-Knoxville and trusted God to make me an instrument in His hand. I was hungry. I was humble. I was young enough. What a time to be alive!

ASK YOURSELF:

- Over the next 5 years, how do I want my life to impact eternity?

- What excuses am I tempted to offer God when He asks for my obedience?

- Have I ever had a, "perhaps you were made for such a time as this" moment? How did I respond?

- How is God asking me to lead through influence today?

- Am I currently working on my resume or toward my eulogy?

- What small efforts of influence can I sacrificially step into now, knowing God will grow that over a lifetime to produce eternal life change in others?

CHAPTER 7
HUMBLE AND HUNGRY

On my first visit to Traders Point Christian Church near Indianapolis, Indiana where my wife grew up, I heard they were giving out free t-shirts to guests. I'm a sucker for free shirts, so naturally, I walked over. I've been given enough church shirts in my day to know that most are pretty lame. They work as free advertising by making you a walking billboard for a church you may not even attend. My expectations were low to say the least, but free is free!

Much to my surprise, as I reached into my "first-time guest" goodie bag, I pulled out a soft, graphic t-shirt with the skyline of Indianapolis imprinted on it. Three massive words, "Humble And Hungry" were plastered on the front of this trendy tee. At first, I chuckled. Humble And Hungry. It seemed like a slogan better fit for a basketball team defending a championship than for an urban church.

Over the next few months, every time I wore the shirt, I saw these three words: Humble And Hungry. They were growing on me so I looked into the intention of Traders Point in making these words their slogan. What I discovered was an attitude of thankfulness for where they have been and a drive to press ahead for more.

I then realized how the phrase "Humble And Hungry" wasn't

just for accomplished athletes with a chip on their shoulder. "Humble And Hungry" is for the church. It should be our battle cry as we declare how much God has done, and remind ourselves how much more He wants to do. I began not only to wear the shirt but to ask myself if I was humble and hungry.

CRAVING THE RIGHT FOOD

In the world of competition, hunger wins every time. It compels people to do desperate, unthinkable things. Hunger drives competitors to train and sacrifice their bodies for victory. A hunger for drugs can cause people to steal, lie and ruin all relationships. An appetite for food compels someone to hunt down a White Castle burger late at night, no matter the inconvenience. Some hunger for approval and are willing to debase themselves and do whatever it takes to receive it. Revenge, comfort, proving someone wrong, and hunger for position all are things that drive some of us toward action.

Something gets you up in the morning and keeps you up at night. All of us hunger for something more than we currently are or have. What motivates you? What compels you to act? This drive to satisfy an appetite deep inside you is a good, God-given trait. The key is making sure we hunger for the right things.

John chapter 4 relates the account of Jesus' interaction with the Samaritan woman at the well. After a long morning of travel, a thirsty, weary Jesus rests there while His disciples go into town to find food. When they come back, they urge Jesus to eat. They figured He was exhausted from all His travel and a quick lunch would restore His energy. Besides, they just made a significant effort to get this food so eating it would at least show a bit of appreciation.

After they pressed Him to eat, Jesus, in typical fashion, gives an unexpected answer. Instead of reaching for a quick lunch and saying, "Thank you," Jesus utilizes the situation to teach about hunger and satisfaction.

He tells them, "I have food to eat that you know nothing about." (v.32)

Understandably, His disciples are now very confused. They proceed to ask each other, "Could someone have brought him food?" They probably had more questions than are recorded in these verses. I can think of a few: "Where in the world did He get this food? Did the Samaritan woman feed Him? If so, why would Jesus accept food from a woman such as that? Has Jesus been holding out on us? Why did we walk all the way into town and spend all that money if He already had something to eat?"

I'm sure Jesus was quite entertained by their confusion and guesses. If it were me, I would have sat there listening to them with a smirk on my lips. But Jesus finished this quick lesson by saying, "My food is to do the will of him who sent me and to finish his work." (v.34)

Suddenly, the disciples realize Jesus is not talking about actual food for the belly. He's giving another glimpse into His heart and the motivation that drives Him to labor so hard, day after day. Like a man starving for a morsel, Jesus will do anything to do the will of His Father. Something had to be driving a man to live as relentlessly as Jesus, to walk hundreds of miles a month, to serve thousands of people a year, and ultimately choosing to die for the same people who wanted to kill Him. Clearly, Jesus was deeply motivated, and for the first time, his disciples got a clear glimpse of what drove Him.

Jesus did not gain His strength and satisfaction from bread and water. Refreshment to continue the journey couldn't be found in something that needed to be digested. Jesus both hungered for and was sustained by something more. The sustaining will of His Father and a burning hunger to finish His work was the only thing that would strengthen Him through His journey to Calvary. This better food ultimately satisfied when He finally could exclaim from the cross, "It is finished." Until then, Jesus always hungered for more.

Ironically, the very thing you believe satisfies is that for which you will continually hunger.

If you seek satisfaction in your accomplishments, you'll do whatever it takes to earn a pat on the back. If it comes from comfort, you'll oddly work tirelessly day in and day out, to secure the ability someday to relax. Maybe you want to be known and accepted, so you work to attain a particular body image or social status so others will admire and want to be like you.

We hunger with a God-given appetite, but we mistakenly try to satisfy that hunger with things that are not true food. If you seek pleasure, comfort or acceptance outside of the Lord and His will for your life, you will never be full. You will always be settling for something less and be deceived into believing you are satisfying a hunger that merits your efforts. Too often we gorge on special treats or sweets that will never fill us up or keep us nourished. As good as the first piece is, could you live on chocolate pie?

Because we are spiritually malnourished, our improperly motivated hearts don't see our God-given tasks through to completion. We weaken and falter, eventually giving up. Why? We haven't hungered for the right thing. We can't be sustained when the work gets hard, because we don't see His will as both our incentive and source of sustenance.

C.S. Lewis puts it like this: "It would seem that our Lord finds our desires not too strong, but too weak…We are far too easily pleased."[1] When we settle for weak desires, we will have weak appetites. These weak appetites will improperly motivate us as we acquire and accomplish things that mean absolutely nothing eternally. Because we are seeking the wrong food, we will be too malnourished to be sustained for what really matters. We are far too easily pleased.

The disciples learned a valuable lesson that day. When nothing in this world can provide the motivation necessary to keep you going for a lifetime, a hunger to finish the work God has given you can see you though. He is the one who will provide you with purpose worthy of your sacrifice. He is the one who ultimately will nourish your soul.

For what do you hunger? What nourishment keeps you going?

Compliments, comfort and criticism may give you a quick burst of energy, but they will never sustain you when real work is required. True food, good food, not only satisfies you in the moment but sustains you through the grind of life. Ultimately you must ask yourself, "Do you hunger to do the work of God?" Is that what rousts you early in the mornings and drives you to finish each day strong? Do you find refreshment and satisfaction from loving God and loving others? Are you satisfied in knowing that God is using your efforts for eternal glory? Until we hunger for substantial food, we will never be motivated to see our tasks through.

SATISFIED BUT STARVING

The good news of the Gospel frees us from the burden of work so we can freely work. We no longer hunger to be accepted by God, as we are stuffed with grace. We labor from a position of acceptance. We find satisfaction not in our accomplishments, but in our position as a child. From this position, our hunger now is to work beside our Father. We hunger to be about the work of the One who saved us. *The paradox of the Gospel is that we have enough in Christ Jesus, yet we always want more—more of Him in our lives, more of Him in the lives of others.*

Jon Acuff suggests we are too easily pleased with lesser things because, "We live in an age with bottomless opportunities and endless distraction."[2] How true is that? We enjoy more resources and opportunities than any other time in the history of the world. From online classes and eBooks, to social media and internet driven small businesses, technology has created both opportunities and distractions for all of us.

While all these resources should equip us to make a positive difference in the lives of others, they instead distract us because we do not hunger for God's work. We rarely see anything through.

Conviction comes often. Inspiration soon follows. Action is seldom taken. Perseverance is hardly experienced. We just move on to something new when it gets difficult instead of putting in the work to complete our God-given opportunity.

We have a perseverance problem, and the root cause lies deep within our motivation. Activity without motivation will always lead to exhaustion. Without a deep hunger, your initial action will simply deplete your energy and leave you vulnerable to fatigue. You will be tempted to quit and turn your attention to another of the many opportunities in front of you or worse, indulge in the endless distractions. Before you know it, you look back and realize you haven't finished anything challenging in years. Your lack of true hunger and satisfaction with dessert has excused you from working to overcome hurdles along the way.

More often than not, you will do whatever motivates you most. All of us are motivated to do something. Some are motivated to scroll through Instagram. Others are motivated to get into God's word. Some are motivated to watch The Office on Netflix for the fourth time. Others are motivated to exercise. What we must realize is that perceived worthiness drives motivation. When you see something as worthy, you will be motivated to act.

Imagine an overweight, middle-aged man who has been trying half-heartedly to shed pounds for years. He's explored various diet fads and the occasional workout routine with some success, but he never saw any of them through when things got hard. He wasn't motivated. Eventually, he becomes content with his level of discomfort.

Then one day his doctor gives him a new perspective when he tells the man his children won't have a father in five years if he doesn't lose 50 pounds. Suddenly he is motivated. In the past, losing weight wasn't worth the effort because he'd rather enjoy his current eating habits than do the work to lose a few pounds. His food and sedentary lifestyle meant more to him than breathing easier or looking better. However, when he realized there was more at stake than how his clothes fit, he had no problem giving up some unhealthy eating habits to be alive and well for his children. Properly motivated, he transformed good intentions into sustained action, because his children are worth it.

Worthiness drives motivation. Behind every action is a motivation that merits the sacrifice. As soon as it is no longer worth it, you won't continue. Instead, you'll start focusing on some other shiny object that has drawn your devotion.

Right now, in your life, what is worthy of your sacrifice? Who or what is worth your perseverance? We will never hunger for what is best until we are motivated by that which is most worthy.

When we fail to continue the work that God laid out for us, it's because we are not motivated by His worthiness. God is worthy of our actions, not just our intentions and when we fail to put our convictions into effect, it reveals what we really think of Him. If you are in Christ Jesus, you should be the most motivated person on the planet! You should be hungry for more! Why? Worthiness drives motivation and our God is most worthy. Nothing before time, in the present, or after time will ever exist that is more worthy. More than improving your health for your child's sake, or proving a person wrong who didn't approve of you, God's worthiness motivates us to hunger for more and to see it to completion.

I believe there are two main reasons why God is worthy of our entire lives.

First, God is best and everything else is less. David reminds us this as he burst out in praise in Psalm 145:3, "Great is the Lord and most worthy of praise; his greatness no one can fathom."

David knows God's greatness is his motivation to praise Him! His entire life was marked by worship as he gave God his "yes" and lived for Him. Who else would he live for? Why would he cheat himself of living for anyone but the best? If at most, we have a few dozen years left on this earth, why would we waste it living for anything else that is a distant second, at best?

Second, serving Jesus is worth it because it is the only thing that produces an eternal reward.

> Bondservants, obey in everything those who are your earthly masters, not by way of eye-service, as people-pleasers, but with sincerity of heart, fearing the Lord. Whatever you do, work heartily, as for the Lord and not for men, knowing that from the Lord you will receive the inheritance as your reward. You are serving the Lord Christ. (Colossians 3:22–24)

Sometimes the people around us don't seem worthy of our efforts. Honestly, that may be true. Too often I do something I think is special and no one notices. At work, I go above and beyond, and no one says, "Thank you." At times, I give a chunk of my hard-earned money to a person or a ministry, and then I feel like they don't use it well. I want to say, "If these people don't appreciate and utilize my efforts and sacrifice, I'm not going to do it anymore. They aren't worth it."

And you know what? Many times people simply aren't worth your efforts. But even if it doesn't seem worth investing your time and attention into their lives, we must realize God is the one who is worth it! And His grace for them, and for you, makes them worth it, too.

Paul makes it clear you aren't doing good things just for them. You do it first and foremost for God who uses your efforts in a way that goes beyond what you could imagine. So, when people aren't worthy, God is!

When we can make that shift and begin doing everything for Him, we will discover a deeper motivation, a motivation sustained by the worthiness of the source of our efforts. God is always worthy.

The encouraging part of serving a worthy God is that He also promises a reward for our efforts. The reward probably isn't going to come from the people we serve but is guaranteed by God who called us. We work not just for satisfaction in this world, but for the promise of the next. None of our efforts for God are in vain because He is using them to eternal benefit. God is worthy of our best because He is the only one who can produce a result and reward every single time! None of our efforts are wasted by God.

THE END IN MIND

If you are in Christ Jesus, success will never define you, but you should be able to define success.

Take comfort in knowing we ultimately are defined, not by what we do, but by what God says about us. We are "human beings," not "human doings." Nonetheless, you don't want to live without a clear definition of success or you'll miss the chance to hunger properly from a satisfied position in Christ. We must clearly know and act on what it means to do the will of Him who has sent us and to finish that work, just as Jesus did. This is only possible if we know the end goal of what God is laying on our hearts.

For Jesus, it was Calvary and nothing was going to stop him from getting there. When others tried to elevate him to earthly kingship, He retreated. When Peter tried to stop him from going to Jerusalem to suffer, He rebuked him. Everything in Jesus' ministry was with the God-sized end goal of bringing salvation to the entire world. He wouldn't settle for the much easier task of healing, feeding and leading a few thousand people to stir up dust in the desert. He knew what it meant to finish His work. He knew what it would require, and He knew the result.

Right now, I want you to think about change you want to see in the world around you. What needs to be different? Safer neighborhoods? Less domestic violence and drug abuse? Fewer suicides among high school and college students? Homeless men and women empowered to use their God-given gifts and abilities to give back to the community?

Take a moment to focus on what God has given you a heart to do and then put an end goal to it. What is the Calvary you are journeying toward? What is the finish line you will tenaciously work toward until you, too, can say, "It is finished"?

For now, don't worry about the "how." Simply picture the "what." What is the win? What needs to be achieved for you to be able to say that you finished the work God had for you?

The reason I don't want you to think about the *how* quite yet is because *how* too often keeps us from considering the first step of *what* needs to change. When we think of the *how* before the *what*, the challenges of *how* keep us from picturing and embracing the God-sized end goal that needs to happen. We delay the work or throw up our hands and never start it because we don't quite know how to address the *how*.

Here is my encouragement. You don't need to know every step of the process. You just need to know the next step and the end goal. Determine what needs to happen and then just start the journey one step at a time. God has a habit of telling His people the *what* and asking them to trust Him with the *how*.

He told Abraham He was going to make his descendants into a great nation, but He didn't say how. God just told him the first step of packing up his things and leaving to a place he would be shown. Jesus told Peter He would build His church on his leadership but didn't tell him how. He simply told him his next step was to tell no one that He was the Messiah and to follow Him to Jerusalem.

This is also how the church I lead operates! We know the end goal is to see our entire community transformed by the power of Jesus. We will not settle for just another service time or a bigger building as the *what*. Those are a part of the process of reaching our end goal, but they are too shallow to be accomplishments on their own. We want to see so many lives changed that our city changes with it! Even though we don't exactly know how that's going to happen, we never take our eyes off the end goal. From there, we simply ask for guidance from God and take our next step in the process.

YOUNG ENOUGH

When you take on this next step mentality, your excuse of being too young flies out the window. You are never too young to start the work the Lord has given you! Doing the work of the Father has no age requirement. We truly are young enough to begin God-sized works, knowing that God chooses to work through us, one step at a time.

I actually think God loves to work through young and underqualified people because their default position is humility. When you have nothing to stand on but the Lord, He will always be the one you go to for guidance, strength and provision. You will pray with desperation because you know if He doesn't show up, you're in trouble. Ultimately, all glory goes to God as God-sized things start occurring for which you could never take credit.

When we get a little older and more experienced, when we're a bit more accomplished and confident in ourselves, we tend to drift from humility and dependence into self-reliance. If you want to settle for man-sized goals, start trusting in yourself more than in the Lord. If you want to stay the course of God-given work, depend on Him daily.

When we first started our church in Gray, we had nowhere to go but to Jesus for everything. Our entire leadership team was under age 30 and had no formal ministry experience. We had hardly any money. We held services in a miserable building. Many of us weren't even from the community we were trying to transform. It was easy for us to humbly and regularly come to God and ask for help with a sermon, finances, or opportunities to serve in the community. Because we couldn't manufacture any of these things, we were forced to rely on the Lord.

Ah, but when God begins blessing, it's easy to begin trusting in yourself, feeling you were somehow responsible for your success. We begin to be satisfied instead of hungering deeply for more. Even today I must fight this! I must stay hungry and come to Him daily asking for more, knowing that all good things only come from Him.

OWED NOTHING. ASK FOR EVERYTHING.

"But he gives us more grace. That is why scripture says: 'God opposes the proud but shows favor to the humble.'" (James 4:6)

When I read James 4:6, two things come to mind. First, I never want to be in opposition to the Lord. Second, I would love His favor. James and Peter both quote this Proverb (Proverbs 3:34) that reveals the heart of God. Our God loves to bless, provide and be for those who have a humble heart. God opposes the proud and seeks to humble them.

A hunger for the Lord's work only honors God when we keep an attitude of humility. Self-sufficiency is the surest way to accomplish nothing significant. As soon as you start taking credit for those things that only He could have accomplished, you are in trouble. The moment you stop asking Him for your daily bread, you are sure not only to lose your hunger but also your provision. We will receive the power needed to see this God-sized work through only when we take the attitude of Paul when he says:

> But he said to me, "My grace is sufficient for you, for my power is made perfect in weakness." Therefore, I will boast all the more gladly about my weaknesses, so that Christ's power may rest on me. (2 Corinthians 12:9)

It is when we begin to live out the ancient saying of Ignatius to, "Work like it depends on you; pray like it depends on God" that God sees our work through. We are hungry enough to do all we can, but humble enough to know it's not sufficient. More than anything, we need God to show us favor. So, we humbly come to Him, asking for our daily bread, pleading for Him to show up. We haven't settled for a task that is humanly possible. We have ventured into a challenge that requires favor of the Lord. So, we ask boldly.

One day I was eating breakfast and sharing Bible insights with a friend at McDonald's when a homeless young man came up to us and asked us for some money. I told him I'd be glad to buy him breakfast but first asked him to sit down so I could hear his story. The 19-year-old young man began to tell me of how he had been through more in the last five years than any person should have to endure in a lifetime. After talking to him for a few minutes, I gave him $20, told him to order whatever he wants, and invited him to come back and join my friend and I as we continued our Bible study.

Five minutes later, he returned with a breakfast spread that could have fed all three of us. As I surveyed the tower of pancakes, biscuits, gravy, eggs and sausage, I saw a look of shame in his eyes. He quickly apologized and explained that he hadn't had anything to eat since lunch the day before and was starving. He didn't know if he'd eat again today, so he wanted to be sure to fill up now. After that, he gave me only eight dollars back in change and apologized again.

To be honest, I was pretty shocked that someone would even attempt to eat 12 buck's worth of breakfast at McDonald's. I quickly told him to enjoy his breakfast and again invited him to join our discussion.

Over the next 30 minutes, I watched this 150 lb., 19-year-old demolish two breakfast platters, a sausage biscuit, Frappuccino and hash brown. He continued to share his story and thanked me and my friend who gave him some money for food later. Before leaving, the three of us prayed that God would continue to become more real in our lives.

The young man I met that morning was hungry, I mean really hungry. A hunger gripped him that I've never experienced and the only way he would be filled was by humbly asking for grace, so he asked. He was met with a gift in the form of $20 and was smart enough to take full advantage of it! He couldn't afford not to. I like to think it was because he trusted me that he bought so much.

Either way, he knew what it meant to be humble and hungry in its most literal sense.

That young man taught me a lesson on grace that day. He taught me how the hungrier you are, the more you should ask for. He helped me experience the joy the Father feels when He gives abundantly more than we need if we will humble ourselves and ask for it all.

Our Father loves providing for those who humble themselves enough to depend on Him. Jesus makes this clear when He says, "If you, then, though you are evil, know how to give good gifts to your children, how much more will your Father in heaven give good gifts to those who ask him!" (Matthew 7:11)

God's grace means holding nothing back. He isn't trying to give you just enough to get by. How often are we crippled by hunger pains, yet only accept a snack? God, who has so much more than 20 bucks to offer, tells us to get whatever we want! His grace is abundant, so He isn't worried about you spending it all. He wants to do great things for His children who humbly come to Him. But instead of ordering a breakfast platter and a Frappuccino, we insult God by choking down a dry biscuit and offering Him change. We ask for just enough to take the edge off our hunger, instead of allowing Him to meet our every need.

I was taught from a young age not to be greedy. When someone is buying your meal, you are to order water to drink and the cheapest thing on the menu. That may be a good practice among friends, but not with God. When God is buying, I want a feast! Anything He offers, I want it! I want my eyes to be bigger than my stomach. I want to be so hungry that I ask for and eat more than I ever have. Like the prophet Elisha, I want to ask for a double portion of God's Spirit. Like Solomon, I desire all the wisdom God can give me. Like the Canaanite woman in Matthew 15, I don't want to leave Jesus' side until He has heard my request. And I don't want any of these things just for myself. I want them so I can finish the work the Lord has given me. If I don't have them, I won't be able to and I'm done trying to manufacture provision for myself.

Too often we don't ask for more because we're not hungry enough. Once we increase our appetite for the work God has given us, like the young man at McDonalds, we can't help but humbly ask for all God will give us to finish the task. Only when you are starving for more of God's work will you humbly ask for His provision.

When we reach this point, not only does God load our plate with more than we can eat, He tells us there's no need ever to apologize for taking what He freely offers. Like the young man at McDonalds, when we humbly ask for help, we not only experience the joy of provision, but we get to enjoy dining with our Provider.

YOUR NEXT STEP

To be a part of God-sized work, humility is a must. It's not about you. You must seek and depend on Him every step. It's not unusual to have no clue how the final step will be accomplished. It seems nearly impossible to envision from the starting point. You must be humble enough to trust God with the unknown and hungry enough to settle for nothing less than finishing the task God has given you.

As long as we stay focused on the goal, and are sure of the next step, we keep moving, knowing that our God secures our footing with each step.

If you wait until you are older and feel more prepared, there is a great chance you will never actually take that first step. Even worse, you may take it without humbly recognizing your total dependence on God because now you give yourself some credit for accumulated wisdom. We must know the end goal for the task God is laying on our hearts and be thinking about *what* is next. You trust Him that all those *how* steps in the middle may require humble sacrifice, but you give Him your willingness. You take a step out of the boat, trust Him to qualify you as you go, and never take your eyes off the goal.

What has God given you a hunger to accomplish? What is your next step to see that end goal reached? Maybe it's to pray for God to give you more hunger for His work. Maybe it's to see Him as so worthy, that your motivation carries you through the uncertainty and sacrifice. How can you humbly ask Him to make a way where currently there is no way?

Although you may be underqualified or under age, you know the end goal and you know the God who will nourish each step. You know that all you can do for now is take that next step, so start there. You trust your hunger for God and know the Lord's provision will carry you through the unknown. You are young enough. Don't wait another day to take your next step.

ASK YOURSELF:

- For what do I hunger? Who or what am I tempted to go to for nourishment and provision?

- The paradox of the Gospel is that we have enough in Christ Jesus, yet we always want more of Him in our lives. Would I say I hunger for more of Jesus? Or am I stuffed, bloated and satisfied with the petite portion of God that I possess, when God is asking me to hunger for more of Him?

- How have I slipped into the routine of being content, when God invites me to pursue much more?

- What tasks remain to be achieved before I can say that I finished the work that God had for me?

PART 4
EXPERIENCED ENOUGH

CHAPTER 8
QUALIFIED BY OUR PAST

PAST MISTAKES. FUTURE GLORY.

"God didn't want me here, but God wants to use me here," said my friend Jahmar, whom I mentioned back in chapter 4. As soon as he said that, I couldn't help but smile and exhale. Jahmar was facing years of jail time, and we had been waiting anxiously to find out just how many.

As you would expect, most of our prayers had been for him to be released as soon as possible to start his new life following the Lord in the "real world." I completely had dismissed the fact that God had a work for him to do on that side of the bars.

As I processed the truth of Jahmar's declaration, I experienced a precious emotion that had eluded me over the past year: contentment. Jahmar helped me exhale and rejoice in the Lord as I finally began to trust that God truly has a plan for my friend. For the first time, I understood that no matter how long Jahmar was to spend in prison, he would be experiencing the joy of finishing the work God had given him. I began to believe that God can and will work through Jahmar, no matter where he is.

Jahmar, a young man who had been following Jesus for just a

few months, already had been freed from his past. Jesus had replaced his condemnation with qualification. He began to teach me how qualifying even our mistakes can be.

The most debilitating lie the enemy wants us to buy is that our past mistakes should keep us from future glory. We begin to believe the deceit that our mistakes limit what God can do through us for the fame of His name. We all have made mistakes that, on our own, could never be crafted into something beautiful. But we are not on our own. We have a Redeemer who shapes those shortcomings into the very qualifier that makes us competent to work.

Jahmar knew God had a much better original plan for his life than spending months in jail. That's a no-brainer. But Jahmar also understood that through this broken situation, God was working. God loved Jahmar enough to use his past to bring him to a point of brokenness so that the Gospel was finally good news to him. Now, Jahmar is the Lord's forever! With that motivation, he isn't going to waste another day living for anyone but Jesus.

Week after week, Jahmar would tell me how he could not wait to get back to his friends, family and community to share his story. He so badly wanted to help them know Jesus and experience life change as he had. He would tell me how he yearned to invest in the younger generation to keep them from living an empty life that could land them in jail, too.

Even in his desire to be used by God outside of jail, Jahmar realized the opportunity he has now while he is behind bars. He could help bring life change to a unique group of broken men who are just as full of potential as he. Because of that, it only took a few months for Jahmar to see the importance of investing in his cellmates while still in jail!

Jahmar knew from experience that the opportunity to know and love Jesus includes those "serving time." God's Spirit was changing lives in that correctional facility. Jahmar's mistake had actually qualified him to be in a unique position to bring life change not just when he got out, but right here and right now. Knowing that, he wasn't going to wait another day to start sharing his story.

His criminal record will keep Jahmar from qualifying for a lot of things. Getting certain jobs will be difficult from now on, if not impossible. He'll have to wait to vote and probably will never be able to own a gun. Unfortunately, some churches may even deny him opportunities to serve and lead. He will suffer future consequences because of past mistakes.

However, because of Jesus, even our mistakes qualify us for great things. Because of Jesus, Jahmar's time in jail cannot be considered a waste.

I reminded Jahmar that while he is in jail, he can be a light in one of the darkest places in our city where few people have access and credibility. He has experiences and a story to share with others that I don't! I can't relate to others who grew up without a father. I can't share about the pressures of trying to find belonging in a tight group of friends who put you in bad situations. I can't empathize with the struggles faced in prison. But Jahmar can!

Not only does he have a story of past pain, struggle and mistakes, but he now has a story of hope, peace and purpose that Jesus brings. He has a story of overcoming addiction and repentance from living for himself. He has found both eternal purpose and current contentment. He can declare he is changed and changing still. No one can stop him from sharing his story. He is ready to use his past, now, for God's glory in the future.

I started visiting Jahmar to minister to him. Now he is the one who reminds me of God's promises and goodness every time I see him. Jahmar is living proof that "God's word is not chained." (2 Timothy 2:9)

What mistakes in your past are you tempted to believe disqualify you? How could God actually use those mistakes and their consequences to spotlight His glory in your life?

Maybe years ago you made the heart wrenching decision to abort your child and God wants to use that mistake to qualify you to walk with women currently considering abortion who need support, strength and wisdom. He wants you to reject guilt, know you are forgiven and choose no longer to feel shame. From this position, you are now free.

Possibly you made financial mistakes that landed you in living conditions of which you are ashamed. Instead of a lovely house in a safe and friendly neighborhood, you live in dilapidated apartment with thin walls and a busted heater, surrounded by broken people. You want to get out of there as quickly as possible, but maybe God wants you to invest in the lives of your neighbors. Even though you never planned to be there, maybe God wants you to choose to live amid the brokenness.

Perhaps you are working at a poverty wage job. Even though you may be tempted to feel defeated, great purpose abounds! Does God want you to stay there simply to finish the work of sharing Jesus with your coworkers before moving on to something else? Instead of seeing your job as a means to a paltry paycheck, God wants you to be intentional and be a light to those with whom you work.

Life does not go as planned. Sometimes that's a direct result of our own sin. Other times it is a by-product of living in a broken world. The good news is that the place you feel trapped is the place where God wants to use you. You may say, "Buddy, you don't know what I've done and where I'm at." That's likely true, but I promise you it's never too late and you are never too far gone to return to God's plan for your life![1] We serve a God who chooses those with a tattered past, to share their current story for His future glory.

REDEMPTION

People love it when something ugly is transformed into something beautiful. That's why shows like Bad Ink gain a following. Bad Ink, originally airing on A&E, followed tattoo artists in Las Vegas who specialized in cover-up tattoos. People come to these artists sporting botched, misspelled, ugly tattoos and ask them to transform the mistakes into something beautiful. And you know what, they pulled it off every time! The before and after shots are incredible! You would never know something awful decorated that same skin just hours before.

The skill and creativity required to redeem a massive, inerasable blotch into something beautiful connects with us. Redemption speaks to us profoundly. Most people can admire a creative work crafted on a blank canvas, but if creation is good, how much better is redemption? We feel a deep hope arise when we see a great artist not just create, but redeem something once labeled ruined. We wonder if that can be done in our lives too.

Our God is not only a creator, but also a redeemer. He not only spoke this world into creation but is making all things new. Even though we are the ones who broke it, He is gladly making it right again.

The Lord not only had a plan for our lives before we were born, but He knows how to rewrite our stories when we get off script. He transforms our dissonance into beautiful harmony to complement His original plan, the moment we return to Him.

God could have started over with each of us, sweeping his arm in disgust across the potter's table, knocking the clay pieces into the trash bin. But God loves us enough to redeem our mistakes. Through our redeemed lives, God gains even more glory. He gets to add another title to His long list of attributes: Redeemer. Maybe that's His most amazing characteristic of all.

STORY TELLERS

The scenes we would delete from the tableau of our lives often are those with the most potential to display God's redemptive goodness. Even those things that embarrass us most, of which we are most ashamed, do not cast us so far from God's love we are unable to return to His plan for our lives. He will gladly bring you back on script, no matter your current setting. He is a good Father and a great Writer.

God is still writing each of our stories. He is the only author able to weave our broken lives together into a massive redemption story. Since Genesis 3, that's what God has been doing. We are plopped right into the middle as characters in the most epic story ever told. The story's hero is Jesus and the plot eventually climaxes with God making all things new.

As characters in this drama, we have one role, one job to do. That is to share our stories with as many people as we can! It's really that simple.

People love a good story. As Bobbette Buster says, "Narrative is our culture's currency. He who tells the best story wins."[2] Isn't that true! Next time you're in a group and someone tells a story, notice what happens. Someone else immediately tries to top it. If someone caught a fish, another person tells of hunting Moby Dick. If a somebody ran off the road in his car, soon someone else was in a 10-car pileup. Our lives are a story and we naturally want it to be telling something worth listening to. From our Instagram, to our resume, to our eulogy, all of us want our stories to matter.

Take a moment and think about what story your life is telling. Is it just a fascinating narrative or is it one that points to a hero that can bring true life change? Each of our stories has a hero. That's what makes a good story, the conflict between heroes and villains. But, not all heroes are worth talking about.

Maybe you've made your hero your job, your spouse, your sport, your possessions, or yourself. Your story could include these set decorations that you claim bring you true joy, contentment, purpose and peace. You could build this façade of fulfillment through earthly possessions, accomplishments, and relationships, but is it best? Should we be exclaiming a different narrative with our lives? Should we be pointing others to a hope bigger than ourselves? Is there a better hero to admire?

Our lives are meant to tell a story with Jesus as the central figure, the main character, the hero in our drama. He is the one who brought us a peace that surpasses understanding and a joy unshakable. Jesus has given us a power and purpose we previously could not attain. He is the one in whom we place our trust that one day all things will be made right and every tear will be wiped away. He is the one who has redeemed us to live for something more. Why would our story feature any other hero?

When you read God's Word, you realize the epic story of human history is all about Jesus. The Old Testament establishes the need for a Savior and foreshadows His coming. The New Testament reveals Jesus as more than we ever could have anticipated. It is when we align our stories with God's epic story and allow Jesus to be the hero in our narrative that we begin to impact lives eternally. We don't settle for talking about some false hero who ultimately will disappoint, just as any job, spouse, sport, possession or obsession will. We chose to focus on the unfailing faithfulness of Jesus as He is the one who saves and satisfies. If He has changed your life, that change should be your storyline, with Jesus as the change agent.

I WAS BLIND, BUT NOW I SEE

You can find a great example of telling Jesus centered stories in John chapter 9. Jesus and his closest disciples come upon a man blind since birth. Still captive to cultural and religious perceptions, His disciples assume the man's blindness is caused by sin. They ask Jesus if it was his own sin, or that of his parents that caused it. Jesus explains that neither assumption is true, the man is blind so that "the works of God may be displayed in him." (v.3)

Jesus then heals the man and word gets around that the blind guy now can see. When people asked this previously blind man what happened, he responded, "The man they call Jesus made some mud and put it on my eyes. He told me to go to Siloam and wash. So, I went and washed, and then I could see." (v.11)

This man's life change was obvious. No ophthalmologist could take credit for it. How it happened exactly, the man wasn't sure. But one thing he did know, a man named Jesus was the hero. This blind man didn't give himself or anyone else credit. He didn't prescribe a mud facial or a quick bath in Siloam. Jesus clearly was the focal point of his life change story.

Like many of us, the blind man couldn't explain everything after encountering Jesus, but the most important detail, he stated clearly: "One thing I do know. I was blind but now I see!" (John 9:25) More than just that, Jesus was the one who opened his eyes. Jesus was given credit as the hero. Now that's a good story!

We share our stories to share Jesus. Who else would we talk about? What's more important, more fascinating, more crucial? Nothing manmade could ever surpass the importance of the One who made man. We should never settle for pointing others to anything or anyone, except Jesus. Even the church comes second to Him. *The church is good only because Jesus is best!* The hero will never be a pastor or your circle of fellowship. Our hero established the church by giving His life for it. Our stories are all about the power of the one and only Savior, Christ alone.

When we share Jesus centered stories, we share a hope that is contagious. A hope our world hungers for as they admire a cheap imitation from a distance in nearly every movie produced or novel published. We simply need to help them see through the evidence of our lives that Jesus is the hero they seek.

When you meet Jesus, He gives you eternal purpose. He tells you to make disciples, exclaim the Good News and to share hope. Our story is the biggest tool for the task. Everyone who follows Jesus has a story in which Jesus is the hero. So, everyone is qualified to share about the power of Jesus.

Some stories are dramatic—addicts come clean, suicidal thoughts evaporate, criminals repent, marriages are restored. Others are more subtle. The self-righteous humble themselves, the selfish look outward, and the successful redefine success.

Each of our stories are perfectly different so they can be told at the perfect time to different people. Our stories tell how Jesus helps us overcome mourning, how Jesus gives us peace during financial crisis, how Jesus gives us contentment in a time of aloneness.

Our stories don't just speak to people at the extremes, they speak also to the masses in the middle. People every day need Jesus to be the hero of their everyday lives. It's our job, duty and privilege to declare and demonstrate that He can and will be that hero! If you have a life change story, you have enough to be a life change agent for others. If you don't have a life change story, Jesus can be your hero today! He can be your Savior who saves and sustains you.

The early church did not have a ton of resources. They didn't have the New Testament, as they were still writing it. They had no building to meet in or budget to spend. They had no study books or online classes to equip leaders. They only had two tools—the Holy Spirit, and their own stories. Both of these tools are still available and are enough for us today.

Everywhere they went, they embraced the Spirit's power to lead them to tell of the life change that Jesus brought to them and can bring to others. What they lacked in theological study or established doctrine, they made up for by focusing on Jesus as the hero of their life change. Just like the blind man, they said all they know is, "I once was blind, but now I see." When we point to obvious life change and credit Jesus with all of it, it is difficult for others not to take notice.

LOOKING TOWARDS THE FINAL ACT

Our stories aren't about perfect people and a smooth series of events. They are narratives of mistakes, suffering, persecution and struggle. Our stories are of real-life pain that connects with the real-life struggles of others. Don't whitewash your story.

However, we aren't telling a tragedy. When the curtain falls on the fat lady's song, our drama will not end in disaster. No, our current struggles always include a future hope. Because of that, we look towards the final act that ends like this:

> And I heard a loud voice from the throne saying, "Look! God's dwelling place is now among the people, and he will dwell with them. They will be his people, and God himself will be with them and be their God. He will wipe every tear from their eyes. There will be no more death or mourning or crying or pain, for the old order of things has passed away." He who was seated on the throne said, "I am making everything new!" Then he said, "Write this down, for these words are trustworthy and true." (Revelations 21:3–5)

If Jesus is your hero, not only is your life being redeemed, but you are inching closer to the day where you see all things restored. Jesus will make everything new. As children adopted into the family of God, we have hope. We know our stories are still being written, and while we don't know the details of every scene, we know the ending. Because the current scene in which we live is not the whole story, we refuse to focus on the current chapter, whether good or bad.

Each of us have had scenes, are currently immersed in a scene, or are approaching a scene in our story of great heartache. Death and illness are inevitable. Shattered dreams and injuries come too often. Financial struggle and depression have become normal. As difficult as these scenes can be, it is these experiences that qualify us to speak truth through our stories. As Paul reminded us in his letter to the church in Corinth:

> Praise be to the God and Father of our Lord Jesus Christ, the Father of compassion and the God of all comfort, who comforts us in all our troubles, so that we can comfort those in any trouble with the comfort we ourselves receive from God. (2 Corinthians 1:3–4)

God doesn't orphan us to walk barefoot through this world of broken glass alone. He isn't waiting to join us until He makes everything new. He chooses to walk with us in the brokenness. He comforts us through our troubles until the day comes when we see His face and suffering is no more.

Following Jesus isn't a life without suffering. Following Jesus is a life that has Him with you amongst the suffering. Only when we receive comfort from God are we then able to comfort others with depth and empathy that goes beyond what this world can offer. It is when our stories are littered with the faithfulness of Jesus that we are equipped to walk through future tough times, and to accompany others through similar difficulties.

Then our comfort, our advice, our shoulder to cry on is not theoretical. We can point them to an actual person who has proven through our experience to be enough. Our stories prove His power. Our lives give evidence that Jesus is a hero worthy of our devotion.

How can you begin sharing your story to point others to a God who saves? How have your past mistakes actually qualified you to bring hope to the hopeless? "God wants to use your story for the salvation of the nations," says Laura Story. "Not because of the greatness of your story, but because of the greatness of our God."[3]

Feel God's grace flow through you, freeing you from the bondage of shame, and compelling you toward a bigger purpose. People can wait no longer to hear your story. They are dying for a narrative with a real hero who can save them. *Someday* starts today and it starts simply by telling your story.

If you feel you are totally off script and too far gone for grace, here is one final reminder from Jahmar. "God may not have desired for you to be where you are, but God wants to use you right where you are." Your past is a part of your future story that God is still writing. How will you tell it?

ASK YOURSELF:

- What past mistakes do I believe disqualify me for service?

- How could my mistakes become my biggest qualifier to help point others toward the hope found in Jesus?

- Right now, what story is my life telling? Who is the Hero of my story?

- Who can I begin sharing a Jesus centered story with in hopes of pointing them to a God who redeems?

CHAPTER 9
THE DRY SEASON IS OVER

PUSHING THROUGH THE DROUGHTS

"The dry season is over." That whispered thought resounded as if God Himself shouted it into my mind.

I was in the midst of my monthly half-day of prayer, pouring out my heart to the Lord, when I finally shut up long enough to just listen. Listening to God is never easy for me, especially when I often don't hear much, but I was desperate.

Our church plant had doubled in an average weekly attendance from 25 to 50 over the last year, and God was doing some great work, but I wanted more. I wasn't satisfied with simple addition. I wanted to see lives changing at an exponential rate. We were preparing to move into a much better facility, but I knew that wouldn't build a church. I needed something more from God.

At this crossroad, I had to decide if I was going to continue to be faithful, or subtly slip into dejection. Discouragement and exhaustion were settling in. I asked myself, "Is all of this really worth it?" more regularly. I was at that place where motivation walks toward the horizon and many people see their God-given dream slowly fade away.

At this critical point in my life, God blessed me. He flooded me with encouragement so rich, it sustains me to this day.

"The dry season is over." To hear that message so clearly without a sound being made was new to me. I didn't need my eardrum to be vibrated to know that God was speaking truth into my life.

When Memphis pastor Adrian Rogers was elected president of the Southern Baptist Convention in 1979, he talked with reporters in the spiritually familiar language he would have used with his church members or Christian friends. He frequently mentioned, "hearing from the Lord," or "the Lord told me," this or that. A curious reporter asked him, "Are you saying you heard the audible voice of God?"

"No," Rogers said. "It was clearer than that."

That's how I felt. I've never heard the audible voice of the Lord. You probably haven't either. I often envy the ancient prophets who clearly heard from God. But what I have is even better. I have God's Spirit who solidifies truth in my life and sometimes even blesses me with special revelation of who He is and what He is able to do. That day I received just that.

As I repeated the words in my mind, "the dry season is over," I felt compelled to sketch a baseball field that was off in the distance. I don't typically doodle, but for some reason that day, I felt the need to draw.

I sketched the field, then added a cloud to the picture. Then another. And then another. Before long, I'd drawn an entire sky full of clouds soaking the baseball field in a heavy downpour. Words from one of my favorite worship songs rolled off my lips: "There is a cloud, beginning to swell."[1]

I put down the pencil and began to plead for God to allow me finally to receive His rain (reign). As my own voice broke the silence around me, I cried out in joy and began to worship God for what I knew was promised, certain it was coming, just not yet received. I knew I would continue to press forward with everything within me. The rain was coming.

To start a challenging, God-given task is hard enough. To see it through to completion can sometimes seem impossible. Plans fall apart. Unexpected struggles arise. Results come more slowly than you anticipated. More times than not, accomplishing the work God laid before you will be a lot harder than you assumed. Setbacks, slow progress, mistakes you make will begin to steal your original passion. Doubts start to replace truth. Despair begins to displace hope. Dry seasons are as sure to come as summer follows spring. How we respond during these seasons will determine the extent of our impact here on earth.

Starting our *someday* aspirations is a great first step, but finishing them is the true goal. No one dreams to someday start something. No, we hope to finish it, to accomplish our God-given task. So how do we push through a dry season and cling to the promises of God? How can we be sure we are driving as hard during the droughts as we do in the fruitful seasons?

Let's find an example in a powerful story at the end of 1 Kings 18. In case you're not familiar, this story occurs when the nation of Israel is in the middle of a drought that has dragged on for years. Because Israel had turned its back on the Lord and started worshipping false gods, the prophet Elijah prayed for a drought to sweep the land as punishment. He hoped God's wrath would lead His people to repentance and back to true life.

God answers Elijah's prayer, and water is cut off. The clouds dry up. Fields turn to dust. For years hundreds of thousands of people don't taste dew or rain. Their very lives are threatened. Elijah is no hero in this story.

After about 3 and a half years, Elijah challenges the prophets of the false gods to an old-fashioned fire calling contest. After Elijah exposes these prophets and their gods as phonies by calling down fire onto a sacrifice that they failed even to create a spark on, he has them exterminated. Now that the worship of false gods is cleaned up within the country, Elijah decides it is time for the drought to end.

> And Elijah said to Ahab, "Go, eat and drink, for there is the sound of a heavy rain." So Ahab went off to eat and drink, but Elijah climbed to the top of Carmel, bent down to the ground and put his face between his knees. "Go and look toward the sea," he told his servant. And he went up and looked. "There is nothing there," he said." (1 Kings 18:41–43)

Before the first cloud appears in the sky, Elijah tells Ahab, King of Israel, to go ahead, eat and drink, because the rain is coming. Think about the significance of this invitation. It hasn't rained for over three years and now you're being told to throw off the shackles of your reservation, of your rationing and to celebrate with eating and drinking. If rain doesn't come, you could burn through your rations and, ultimately, starve. Ahab wasn't a big fan of Elijah, but he was a fan of self-indulgence, so he scurried home to feast for the first time in a long time. But not Elijah. He had work to do.

Elijah climbed to the top of a mountain. Isn't that where all good prayers are prayed? He put his face in between his legs as if bracing for impact on a plummeting airplane, and prayed for rain. What he said to God, or how long he pled it, we don't know. But after some time, he looked up and told his servant to check to see if the rain was coming. This prayer and plan worked to stop the rain, why wouldn't it work to bring it back? Moments later, the servant reports…nothing. Nada. Zip. Not even a cloud.

If I were Elijah at this point, I'd be a little frustrated. He had served God long and well. He trusted God enough to ask for a drought because he wanted God's people to turn back to Him. He was confident that was best for Israel and that God would again bring rain in due time.

As you can imagine, Elijah was not very well-liked. Bringing drought to an entire country doesn't get you invited to many dinner parties. In fact, many people wanted his bones to rest with his ancestors for what he had done. To further threaten the proximity of his head to the rest of his body, he just promised King Ahab some rain. If God doesn't deliver, Elijah has to answer to Ahab. With all of this swirling around in his mind, Elijah does what he knows to do. Instead of becoming dispirited, frustrated and losing sight of his goal, like too many of us do, he goes right back at it and continues to pray.

Again, he tells his servant to check. Again, a bad report is delivered. This pattern continues a few more times and Elijah refuses to take "no" for an answer.

This short, intense, but neglected account in Israel's history can't be overlooked, because it shows us the importance of perseverance. Elijah demonstrates how confidence in our calling should sustain us through the droughts. He knew God wanted him to pray for a drought. He also knew God would honor his obedience by causing the rain to return when the time came.

Elijah wasn't going to panic or run off course from the game plan. If God wanted him to pray, he would continue to pray. If the first prayer honored God, how much more did the seventh? As Pastor Mike Todd simply puts it, "Anything worth doing, is worth doing continually."[2] Elijah knew that asking God for rain was worth doing the seventh time just as much as it was the first. He refused to be discouraged by the lack of immediate results. He stayed the course and one more time he prayed and sent his servant to check.

"The seventh time the servant reported, 'A cloud as small as a man's hand is rising from the sea.'" (v.44)

There is a cloud beginning to swell! When I read verse 44, I can't help but stick my hand out, close one eye, and imagine a small cloud in the sky the size of my fist. I can almost guarantee you are doing the same thing right now as well.

I'm no meteorologist, but I know that a puny cloud that size isn't enough to soak an area in a three-year drought. Again, if I were in Elijah's situation and my servant told me he could see only a teeny cloud on the horizon, I'd stick my head back between my legs and get back to praying. Obviously, I'd know God needs a little more encouragement to send something worth getting excited about. Not Elijah. His faith was stronger than mine.

> So Elijah said, "Go and tell Ahab, 'Hitch up your chariot and go down before the rain stops you.'" Meanwhile, the sky grew black with clouds, the wind rose, a heavy rain started falling and Ahab rode off to Jezreel. (v. 44–45)

Elijah realized the little cloud was God waving a flag, telling him rain was coming, just as he had prayed. Elijah was so confident in that sign, that before he felt the first drop of rain, he warned Ahab to quickly head home because a storm was about to hit. Can you imagine how foolish this sounded? It hadn't rained in over three years, there is but one small cloud in the sky, yet you are warning the king of a storm to start any minute.

Perhaps the most astonishing part of Elijah's faith was that he didn't need to wait for all the results to recognize that God would keep His promise and see him through. He was confident enough to pray for rain, and to prepare to get wet.

ONE MORE PRAYER

Think how tragic it would have been had Elijah stopped praying after the first or third or sixth time the servant reported no sign of rain. Imagine the disappointment if his faith was only enough to prompt him to start praying, and not enough to persevere. Think how many thousands of lives would have been lost if he took "no" for an answer. What if Elijah didn't stride confidently down the mountain and prepare for the downpour when he saw the first cloud? What a shame if he had died in a storm on that mountain because he didn't trust God's provision.

Too often our faith walks are marked by good intentions, initial action, and then a wilting resolve. How many God-given dreams fall one prayer, one step, one day, one small cloud short of being realized? How many victorious stories of God's goodness are left on the table because His people tapped out too soon? How often do we climb the mountain and pray, but stop knocking before we see the cloud? How common is it for us to see a cloud forming above and instead of rejoicing that help is at hand, be disappointed in its size?

For us to be a *today* people who see our *someday* aspirations through, we must take Elijah's example to heart. Push through until God shows up. Refuse to give up before we have a clear answer.

Hopefully, you will be flooded with the blessing of His favor for which you hope. Other times only a wispy cloud will rise that requires you to trust it signals coming rain. Through this process, your newly learned perseverance leaves you not only with an opportunity to glorify God but also equips you with a new, deeper, personal trust in the Lord.

The words, "the dry season is over" encouraged me during that half day of prayer because, for the first time, I truly understood and believed that God was going to come through. I had changed careers, moved to a new city, labored for thousands of hours, to witness only moderate change. I had seen a cloud starting to swell, but I had lived long enough to know that not all clouds produce a downpour.

And that's what I wanted. I wanted to be drenched beneath an absolute, torrential deluge of God's goodness in our city. But I doubted my leadership was strong enough to help make that happen. After hearing that promise from God, I became confident that my efforts indeed were productive. He was working, I just needed to remain steadfast.

As soon as I felt my confidence return, assured that my efforts would one day show positive Kingdom results, I gained renewed swagger. I spotted the distant cloud. I was energized to work harder even in the mundane responsibilities that God had given me to manage, knowing the rain was coming.

As I write this, it's been a year since that afternoon when I heard from God. And you know what? The flood hasn't come...yet. We've seen some showers; a few dozen people have had their lives changed by Jesus. We've doubled our weekly attendance yet again. New leaders have been identified, trained and sent. Hundreds of hours have been invested in our city.

While the downpour hasn't washed over our city, I anticipate it at any moment. The clouds continue to swell. I no longer wonder *if* it will happen, I just anticipate *when*. Because of that, I will not lose heart. I will take on new challenges and hurdles with confidence in Him. I will remain steadfast in holy anticipation, knowing that God will reward my faithfulness in due time.

It doesn't have to be raining to declare the dry season over. It all starts with a prayer and a cloud no bigger than your fist.

BROKEN DREAMS. OPEN DOORS.

Perhaps the most difficult reality to accept is that our biggest blessings sometimes come through closed doors. Relationships end. Jobs are lost. Applications are denied. Church plants fail. Each of us have at some point felt certain that God was leading down a certain hallway, only to get a door slammed in our face before we reach the room at the end. How would God allow this? Weren't we doing it for Him? Traveling under His direction?

The resounding clang of a slamming door can shatter our confidence gained through previous experiences in which God proved Himself faithful. We question, "How could God not reward those who are trying to live for Him and His Glory? Why should we give God our lives if we are going to be disappointed?"

In these moments we can either give up or take the attitude of Elijah and remain faithful. We must choose to believe that even broken dreams can create open doorways.

Joseph had a dream. A literal dream. A very unique dream. Towards the end of the book of Genesis, you learn that Joseph dreamed there would be a day when his mom, dad, and 11 brothers would bow down to him. That's a pretty audacious claim for the youngest in the family to make. As you can imagine, his brothers didn't take this too well.

You'd probably expect a few harsh words from them and maybe a butt whuppin', but this story in Genesis 37 is much more tragic. Joseph's brothers throw him into a pit to die, before eventually deciding instead to sell him into slavery.

Slave traders take Joseph to Egypt where he eventually finds favor with an influential official. After years of faithful service in Potiphar's household, Joseph lands in jail for a crime he didn't commit. Potiphar's wife frames Joseph for adultery and he spends years in prison, even though he was faithful to do all God asked of him.

At this point in his life, Joseph couldn't have felt further from his God-given dream. However, Joseph didn't stop living faithfully for God and God again blessed him.

After years in prison, Joseph overheard two prisoners discussing their strange dreams. God helped Joseph correctly interpret those dreams and eventually word came to Pharaoh that a Hebrew in Pharaoh's prison had a special gift. Pharaoh was wrestling with a few strange dreams himself and he called for Joseph.

Joseph told Pharaoh his dreams revealed there was about to be seven years of plenty followed by seven years of famine across Egypt and neighboring countries. He said Pharaoh needed to appoint a wise man to help prepare for this famine to save both his citizens and those of surrounding nations. In a drastic turn, Pharaoh appointed Joseph to be that wise man in charge! So Joseph, the youngest brother, sold as a slave, went from a pit, to a prison, to the palace.

Joseph was now second in authority only to Pharaoh in the most powerful nation on earth. He led well and when the famine hit, Egypt was ready. The surrounding nations were not. Thousands of people traveled to Egypt for food and guess who came begging for help? Yes, decades after Joseph's dream, his brothers bowed at his feet, pleading for food to bring back to their family, just as

Joseph had been told would happen years earlier. In one of the most beautiful and ironic masterpieces ever formulated, God saw Joseph's dream through.

Joseph had plenty of dreams dashed and doors slammed before his God-given dream came true. Along the way, it seemed like the harder Joseph tried, the worse his fate. However, the key trait of Joseph was that he did his absolute best, no matter in what circumstance God put him. Every negative experience prepared him for future success. Whether as a house slave, a prisoner, or second in command of an entire nation, Joseph gave all he had to the Lord. He knew that even in mundane, daily tasks, God was working toward something miraculous. He trusted that, as John Newton put it millennia later, "All shall work together for good. Everything which He sends is needful; nothing can be needful which He withholds."[3]

Even though Joseph's dream had a timeline he didn't anticipate and a complexity that must have made him question, he never gave up on God. And God never gave up on him. This attitude sustained Joseph until the end of his life so he could tell his brothers, "You intended to harm me, but God intended it for good to accomplish what is now being done, the saving of many lives." (Genesis 50:20)

God would not settle for Joseph's shallow, even braggadocious dream. He had to crush it ultimately to open the door to a better one, a dream that not only had his brother's bowing at his feet, but saved thousands of lives.

DON'T EVER GIVE UP

"Don't give up, don't ever give up." Those words of North Carolina State University basketball coach Jimmy Valvano have echoed through the decades. In 1993, Valvano received the Arthur Ashe Courage and Humanitarian Award at the ESPYS, less than two months before cancer took his life.

Valvano, who barely had energy to make it through a day, not only traveled to receive the award but gave one of the most passionate and inspiring speeches of the 20th century. During this speech, he announced the launch of the Jimmy V Foundation for Cancer Research and emphasized that he would fight for himself and for others until the day he died. Valvano earnestly asked others to fight alongside him by donating to cancer research as he exclaimed, "It may not save my life. It may save my children's lives. It may save someone you love."

Valvano's life changed drastically when he was diagnosed with adenocarcinoma. His doctor's announcement dashed many dreams and aspirations the moment Valvano learned he had only months to live. But Valvano didn't give up. He knew that God closed one door, simply to open another.

Twenty-five years later, Valvano's legacy lives on as he pushed through the last few months of his life to make more of an impact than in all of his previous years of coaching. His example has encouraged thousands to keep fighting. It's raised over $200 million for cancer research.[4]

Because Valvano never gave up, we are closer to curing cancer every day. Because Valvano never gave up, we are still reaping a harvest from his labor.

The apostle Paul in Galatians 6:9 encourages us to, "not become weary in doing good, for at the proper time we will reap a harvest if we do not give up." Often the most difficult part of following God obediently is trusting that His timing is perfect. We feel the harvest is delayed. We expect fruit too quickly. We want results right now, if not sooner.

Listen, the only way to guarantee that your planting and nurturing efforts will yield a harvest is to refuse to give up! Simply put, to quit is to fail. Though your journey may take a different route than you first imagined and your next step feels like there is no ground beneath your foot, as long as you are willing to take it and are committed to doing good, the Lord of the harvest is at work in your life.

GETTING UP

"...for though the righteous fall seven times, they rise again, but the wicked stumble when calamity strikes." (Proverbs 24:16)

The good news of Jesus verifies the truth that *falling and failing are not the same thing*. While there is only one letter of difference in those two words, the one you identify with will change your life forever.

Maybe you've made a mistake and fallen. That's not a new challenge to God. He has redeemed and reconciled adulterers, murderers, liars, thieves, prostitutes and cowards for His glory. The common trait in these redeemed sinners was that each of them trusted God enough to get up and try again.

Has an unforeseen challenge knocked you down? Get up! The world sees your problem as a setback. God sees it as a setup. You demonstrate the depth of your faith not when you are on your feet, but when you are knocked on your butt.

So yes, there will be times when you must alter your plans, but the overall dream of finishing the work God has given you will remain. Maybe you need to make a few adjustments, maybe you've had a few setbacks. Wherever you are, continue to ask yourself, "What's my next step?" Then, get up and take it! God delights in the one who falls, yet trusts Him enough to get back up and try again. Do you really trust that if you get up, Jesus will hold you steady?

Fullness of life is found in the battle. Intimacy with Jesus is not a self-manufactured feeling. Intimacy comes from shared experiences. You grow closer to Jesus when you walk with Him through the droughts. Better than the rain is the presence of the One who provides it.

You grow closest to God when you are most dependent on Him. You gain a satisfaction from Him that the comforts of our world can never provide. Your ultimate joy isn't in harvesting the fruit. You experience ultimate joy as you labor with our Savior.

EVEN AS WE ARE

It's easy to forget that the heroes of the faith, like Elijah and Joseph, were just like us. James reminds us:

> Elijah was a human being, even as we are. He prayed earnestly that it would not rain, and it did not rain on the land for three and a half years. Again he prayed, and the heavens gave rain, and the earth produced its crops. (James 5:17–18)

Elijah and Joseph walked through years of both disappointment and opportunity, trusting that in their day to day faithfulness, God was at work. We too, have that opportunity. Let our prayers be earnest as we trust that the same God of Elijah answers our prayers and responds to our steadfastness.

There is a cloud beginning to swell. The dry season is over. Trust Him enough to see you through until the rain comes, no matter how long that takes.

ASK YOURSELF:

- What dream am I tempted to give up on that God is asking me to trust Him with?

- How can I embrace setbacks to become setups that equip me for God's future plans?

- In what way is God asking me to persevere through this drought?

- Am I willing to offer one more prayer to see it through? And then, another?

- How can I be satisfied knowing He is with me, and the rain surely approaches, though all I see now is a dusty plain?

PART 5
CALLED ENOUGH

CHAPTER 10
HEARING WELL DONE

EARNING YOUR TITLE

I love walking through cemeteries. That may seem strange, but I think more people should do it. When I walk through the silent rows of stones, each testifying to a life once lived, the inscriptions they bear remind me how we should live our lives to their fullest. Silently, they shout that a day will come when people remember only your name and a line or two chiseled into the stone that will summarize your entire life.

Country singer Garth Brooks sings about this in his song, "Pushing up Daisies." The chorus goes like this: "There's two dates in time that they'll carve on your stone, and everyone knows what they mean. What's more important is the time that is known in that little dash there in between."

Have you ever thought about the words to be written on your tombstone? Maybe you'll never actually have them inscribed as a last message to the world about who you are, but just take a moment to think about it. How would you want your life described in those few words allotted by space on a stone?

Some will declare "beloved husband" or "precious wife." Others may confirm their passion for a hobby or career. Some may even proclaim an inspiring saying such as, "Live, Laugh, Love." All of us want to be remembered for something, even if it eventually is summed up in a few words.

I want to be remembered by only one title. I want two words to come to mind every time someone looks back at my life, or strolls through the cemetery reading headstones. I hope my decades of labor on this side of the veil will culminate in one well earned, all-important title. I pray "Faithful Servant" becomes the two words that any one would think of to describe me when I'm gone. This title can only be earned through a lifetime of faithfulness. It's a title worthy of a life's investment.

In the middle of Matthew 25, Jesus tells a parable of a rich man going on a journey. A parable is a story that Jesus makes up to illustrate a point. In this story Jesus reveals a powerful truth of what our Master in heaven expects of us.

Before he leaves, the rich man in the story meets with three of his servants and gives each of them a large sum of money to manage in his absence. This was a prevalent practice in the absence of a global stock market or certificates of deposit as safe havens in which to invest at that time. Someone with great wealth who was unable to manage it, temporarily would put it into the hands of a trusted colleague to invest.

As you would expect, this master entrusts to each servant a sum based on that servant's ability to create a profit. To the first servant he gives five "talents," which is a measure of weight of gold equivalent to 100 years pay for manual labor.[1] To the second he gives two talents or 40 years salary for manual labor. And to the last servant he gives a single talent, still equivalent to 20 years of his salary.

The master takes off and immediately the two servants with the more substantial amounts get to work. They begin to trade and invest and work hard so that when their master returns, he will be pleased. After what Jesus said was "a long time" of working tirelessly, both of them doubled their investments! The servant with five talents makes an additional five, and the servant with two talents makes two more. These two servants act diligently, promptly and responsibly to do the best they could with what was entrusted to them, and their profits showed that.

Unfortunately, we can't say the same about the third servant. Jesus says that servant simply buried his talent, ensuring that it was kept safe and would not diminish, but also assuring it would not grow.

When the master returns and begins to settle his accounts, the first two servants proudly report their earnings. The master is very thankful and tells each, "Well done, good and faithful servant! You have been faithful with a few things; I will put you in charge of many things. Come and share your master's happiness!" (v.21–23).

These two servants received a great reward! They gained approval and affirmation from their master, a title of "faithful," an increase in responsibility and a portion of the master's happiness. What a reward! I would argue that the significance of these rewards surpasses the worth of the talents gained. Unlike mere gold, these servants had just been given something that could never be lost.

When the third servant comes up to bat to account for his work, he meekly offers his lone talent, seasoned with excuses. Ultimately, he says he was afraid he couldn't meet the master's expectations, so he simply buried the gold instead of risking a loss. As you can imagine, this didn't go over well with the master. He wanted the money put to work! If he wanted it buried, he could have done that himself. The master's response is stern and to the point. Verses 26 and 27 say:

> His master replied, "You wicked, lazy servant! So, you knew that I harvest where I have not sown and gather where I have not scattered seed? Well then, you should have put my money on deposit with the bankers, so that when I returned I would have received it back with interest."

The master then takes the talent from the lazy servant and gives it to the first faithful servant, who already had 10 talents. Next, the master orders the worthless servant to be thrown into the darkness. This worthless servant received no reward. Instead, he was scorned, called "lazy" and "wicked," stripped of his position, and denied the happiness of his master.

WHICH WORDS WILL YOU HEAR?

"Well done good and faithful servant."

At the end of my life, all I want to hear is that sweet phrase from Jesus himself. As great as it would be to hear it on my deathbed from my wife, family, friends and co-workers, they are not my ultimate concern. They've been gracious enough to tell me "well done" my entire life. As much as I appreciate their encouragement, it leaves me unsatisfied because it's not enough to please man. My friends, family and co-workers will never set for me the standard of faithfulness. No matter how high their standard, if I settle for theirs, I will fall short of the real goal—to be declared "faithful" by Jesus.

I am a very goal driven individual. I've been setting goals to reach toward for my entire life. An indescribable rush of positive vibes pours through you when you achieve something for which you've worked hard. After accomplishing hundreds of goals in my lifetime, I've found that the more difficult the goal, the greater satisfaction upon achieving it.

We all are working toward something. It is natural to seek the reward that comes with accomplishment. But are we chasing after the ultimate goal? Are we seeking the true and better reward?

When you mount the podium of life to receive your participation medal the only award that truly matters is the blue ribbon of "faithful servant." All other ambitions you pursue should be steps that set you up to achieve this bigger goal. It is only this prize—hearing those sweet words from our Savior, "Well done good and faithful servant"– that properly rewards your decades of service and sacrifice.

Eventually we will give account of our *someday* aspirations. Our Master is coming back soon, and when He does, we will either proudly tell Him of all that we did, or fearfully fumble with excuses of all we intended to do. The decisions you make now will determine whether or not you hear that proud admonition from the Lord.

Which are you working towards?

NOTHING MORE. NOTHING LESS.

I'm comforted in this parable to see the master giving out responsibility based on his servants' abilities. He doesn't expect an underqualified servant to handle an absurd amount of wealth. He doesn't presume an unrealistic return on a small investment. But, he does give each servant a valuable resource and expects them to multiply it.

As you watch the parable play out, it reveals a special trait about the master. He not only entrusts each servant with some gold, but he genuinely wants to give them more! He isn't focused on his own selfish gain, but he looks forward to the day he can entrust his servants with more purpose and responsibility.

As much as he wants to give them more, he knows the best preparation for success is to start them off with an amount they can handle. This way, he demonstrates his own wisdom in how he invests his resources and that he loves his servants enough to set them up for success.

This perspective of the loving-kindness and wisdom of our Master should help us realize He always gives us the perfect amount of resources to steward. You can exhale and relax a bit as you realize God would never give you more than you are capable of managing with Him by your side. While He loves us enough not to drown us with too much to start with, He also promises to give us more once we show ourselves faithful with what we have been given.

Our hard work will not go unnoticed. We rise to our Master's expectations to steward what we have and make no excuses for what we don't.

As you prove yourself faithful with what you were entrusted, God will give you more. When you truly believe that God has entrusted you appropriately, you will be convinced that today is the perfect day to be faithful. You are never too young or too underqualified to do your best with what you have been given.

Sure, you anticipate one day managing and accomplishing more, but first you demonstrate faithfulness in handling what you have been given now. Trust that God will equip you through day to day obedience. If you want to accomplish great things *someday*, start with faithful execution of the small tasks before you today.

Our problem is that we see whatever talents we've been given as insufficient to do great things. We think, "How in the world could I do anything substantial with this?" We want 10 or 20 talents to manage right now, and instead of working with what we have to show we're worthy of more, we become discouraged and do nothing. We bury our God given resources deep in the earth. Simply put, we are lazy. We may even doubt our master will come back, so we think, "What's the point?"

In these moments our actions, not our words, expose the depth of our faith. Jesus himself says in John 14:12, "Very truly I tell you, whoever believes in me will do the works I have been doing."

If we survey the talents we've been entrusted with and still are not compelled to act, we don't trust God. We don't have faith that doing our best with what He's given us is enough for Him to use. We don't believe that faithfulness with little will give us a chance to be faithful with much.

If we're honest, we know the simple expectation for us in this life is to do the best we can with what we have. We know it is in the hard work of everyday life that we accomplishment meaningful things. But at the end of the day, many of us would rather just be comfortable. We'd rather wait it out and hope our Master will give us a few more talents, even though we've done nothing to earn them.

Instead of obedience, we settle for comfort. We keep thinking of *someday* obeying the God-given tasks in front of us—but not today. Too easily, we begin to consider *someday* an actual calendar entry. More than the sacrifice of faithfulness, we pursue the comfort of procrastination. Even worse, we begin to enjoy it.

We make comfort the ultimate goal of our lives and obedience is an afterthought. We spend our lives making excuses about not having enough, not being enough, to make a difference. So we kill more time working in our own strength to become more qualified or equipped. If we are honest, we are simply justifying our laziness. In the midst of this temptation, we must understand faithfulness.

Faithfulness demolishes the sorry rationale that we don't have enough to make a difference. You don't need a lot to be faithful, you just need something, and we all have *something*. Even if it's only with a single talent to invest or a seemingly menial job to work, we can labor heartily, as for the Lord. Maybe it's just one friend, child, or neighbor to love, we can choose to love them sacrificially like Jesus loves His church. It could be just one week a summer to shed your cultural baggage and travel on mission overseas or one evening a week to serve a local widow and orphan, we can still choose to invest that time with the lost and the least.

When we give God all we have He begins to create returns for our efforts beyond our imagining. God is asking you to offer your best effort, not your best excuse. Why settle for the comfort of coasting over the thrill of investing? If there is one thing this parable is telling each of us, it is that God is not calling us to comfort. God is calling us to faithfulness.

OBEDIENCE > COMFORT

Comfort is temporary and cheap. Obedience to God is eternal and worth our lives. We are obedient not only because it's what's best for us, but because obedience produces fruit in the lives of others, too. But then again, comfort is more appealing than obedience. Taking the comfortable path sometimes produces more immediate results, but they are frail. We sacrifice the power of delayed gratification on the altar of our immediate, selfish desires. Comfort and obedience butt heads. We must choose.

God cares a lot more about your obedience than your comfort because He knows obedience is best. Just like any good father, God will not let his children settle for comfort when there is something better at hand. Think about it. Children are more comfortable playing video games, eating cookies and sleeping until noon, but good parents make them finish their homework, eat dinner before dessert and get up and exercise because they know what's best!

"I don't want to" is never a good enough reason to let a child disobey your clear instruction of what needs to be done. Clearly, as an adult with 25 more years of life experience than the child, you know what is best. God is the same way! He loves us too much to let us tinker with temporary comforts when His eternal purpose is at hand.

Without a doubt, Jesus is the prime example of how we must reject temporary comfort in favor of obedience. Jesus not only commands us to do something but models it for us. Hebrews 12:2 says, "fixing our eyes on Jesus, the pioneer and perfecter of faith. For the joy set before him he endured the cross, scorning its shame, and sat down at the right hand of the throne of God."

Jesus' example of willing obedience should move us to take on the same attitude. The night before Jesus died, He was so distraught about his pending agony that he was literally sweating blood. Demonstrating a condition we now know as hematidrosis, the capillaries that fed into his sweat glands began to rupture, causing blood to excrete from his skin. This rare condition occurs only under very extreme levels of stress. Clearly, Jesus dreaded the discomfort and agony of the cross.

The more comfortable route would have been to deny it, to refuse. Even to call 10,000 angels and throw His Father's plan into disarray. He even asked for a different option if it were at all possible! But ultimately, Jesus trusted his Father. He trusted and loved Him enough to obey Him, even when it was very uncomfortable and the way led to death. Because of this, His response was, "not my will, but yours be done." (Luke 22:42)

Because Jesus trusted and looked forward to a higher joy to come, He endured the discomfort of the cross. He didn't love the shame of the cross as He hung on it naked and abused, but He endured it. He looked beyond it to something better. He focused on returning to the Father. He looked to the freedom his suffering would purchase for all who believe in Him.

His obedience was uncomfortable, but God was faithful to use it! *In Christ, we find the model and the motivation for our obedience.* Our model comes from the One who loved us more than His own comfort. Our motivation is knowing that God never wastes our sacrifice.

"Obedience is our responsibility," said Elisabeth Elliot. "The result of our obedience is up to God." Paul reminds us in 1 Corinthians 3, that God makes things grow. When you look closely at Jesus' parable, you will notice the master commends faithfulness, not the result. His focus is on obedience, not the talents gained. We are rewarded based on our willingness to labor, not on our ability to produce. This takes pressure for results completely off the table and frees us to enjoy watching God work through our efforts.

TRADING GOOD FOR BEST

"Our greatest fear should not be of failure but of succeeding at things in life that don't really matter." — D.L. Moody

When I first read these words written by Dwight L. Moody well over a century ago, regret immediately gripped me. I couldn't help but mourn over all the good things I had lived for. I've pursued success in the classroom, on the basketball court and in my career. From the world's perspective, I am on course to live and die a successful man.

The only hitch is that I've dramatically changed my definition of success. I've replaced the American Dream with the Great

Commission. And now, with this new metric, I must determine if I am actually succeeding at the things that really matter.

I've identified the culprit that tries to block me from earning the title of Faithful Servant—success. It tastes so sweet. It's addictive and makes me keep coming back for more. But now I ask if my successes really matter?

Every time you say "yes" to a *good thing*, you risk having to say "no" to a *God thing*. We continue to put God stuff off for *someday*, because we crowd our lives with good things. Some have said "no" to a mission trip for years because they've been saying "yes" to career, savings or family. Others feel the tug to invite their neighbor over for dinner and initiate a relationship but have settled for a movie night at home telling yourself you're "investing in your family." In the process, you've robbed your family of the joy of making disciples.

For some, it is saying "yes" to starting a different job or changing majors. Others know they should be starting a ministry of their own. The problem is, we aren't willing to say "no" to good things. School, sleep, savings and extra shifts at work have taken priority. We don't have room for another "yes," even if it's to do a God thing.

What do you need to be willing to fail at, to give yourself an opportunity to succeed at what matters most? It could be as simple as being okay with a messy house or as serious as leaving a job. Are you willing to called foolish by the world to be labeled faithful by God? Where have you mismanaged your "yes" at the expense of being faithful to your Savior?

Maybe you've invested so much in your children that you've forgotten to keep obedience to God your top priority. Maybe you are so financially strapped by your standard of living, that you can't say "yes" to moving, switching jobs, giving more, or going overseas to serve the Lord.

Let us be a people who hold precious and protect our "yes" for the One who defines success. Let our faithfulness be born of a willingness to pursue the best, over the good. It is not too late to begin being faithful. To what is God asking you to say "yes" today?

ASK YOURSELF:

- If I died today, would I hear Jesus tell me, "well done, good and faithful servant"?

- What have I overlooked that God is asking me to be faithful with? What is something I've put off for tomorrow, that God wants me to address today?

- How could current faithfulness produce even more opportunity down the road?

- In what ways have I chosen comfort over obedience?

- Are there any good things I need to stop doing so I can make space to take on more God things? Is there a hobby or habit I need to give up to make space for a God task?

CHAPTER 11
THE DANGER OF COMPARISON

COMPARISON KILLS

My competitive nature runs deep and I've been comparing myself to others since I was a child. As soon as I learned to swim, I needed to be faster than my older sister. In school, I needed better test scores than my friends and classmates. Even now, if I am not careful, I begin comparing the growth of the church I pastor to the churches around me. As much as I dislike this about myself, I can't seem to escape it.

Comparison starts as a natural and relatively harmless thing. All of us do it. When you're growing up, are you taller than your older cousin? Did you learn to ride a bike first? Who can hit a 3-pointer more consistently?

Many of us enjoy it. But over time, this instinctive and "harmless" habit can grow into a stifling disease. Who is prettier? Who got into a higher prestige college? Who makes more money, drives a fancier car?

This disease not only will steal your joy, it eventually will kill your calling. Let me explain the danger of comparison.

COMPARING OURSELVES TO THE WRONG PERSON

In Luke 18, Jesus tells another parable. This time his audience is a bunch of self-righteous, religious snobs who trust in their own position more than in God. To expose their wicked hearts, Jesus creates two characters in His story. One is a religious Pharisee—a high profile leader in the synagogue—and the other is a tax collector who makes his living from lying, stealing and exploiting fellow Jews. As contrasting as is their status and style, their current attitudes towards worshipping God are just as different.

> Jesus told this parable: "Two men went up to the temple to pray, one a Pharisee and the other a tax collector. The Pharisee stood by himself and prayed: 'God, I thank you that I am not like other people—robbers, evildoers, adulterers—or even like this tax collector. I fast twice a week and give a tenth of all I get.' But the tax collector stood at a distance. He would not even look up to heaven, but beat his breast and said, 'God, have mercy on me, a sinner.' I tell you that this man, rather than the other, went home justified before God." (Luke 18:10–14)

In this story, Jesus exposes our tendency not only to compare but to compare ourselves to the wrong person. Instead of holding our current spiritual condition up to the light of God's expectations, we settle for comparing ourselves against other sinners.

The Pharisee had a pride issue that kept him from loving God and others. In his arrogance, he compared himself to those around him and came out feeling pretty doggone good. Instead of humbling himself, worshipping God and seeking His kingdom, he found comfort in not being an "evildoer."

Now that sounds absurd, because bragging about not being a bad character, like a robber or adulterer, doesn't seem like a solid patch of proud ground on which to stand. But then we realize we do the same thing.

We look around and notice the negative things others are doing, and are proud that we're "not like that." We compare spiritual report cards and as long as we are beating the curve, we settle. Being better than others by comparison excuses us from pushing ahead. We decelerate as if we've earned rest based on previous accomplishments. Eventually, we drift from faithful moorings and stop saying "yes" to new things Jesus is inviting us into.

Imagine if the five-talent servant in Matthew 25 stopped working hard after his first good investment. It would have been easy for him to compare his earnings to the two talents the other faithful servant made or to the one talent the lazy servant buried, and think that he deserved a break. He'd already produced more than those around him, so why not coast?

The danger here is that when you compare yourself to others, you allow their definition of faithfulness to shape yours. God may have entrusted you with much more and may be expecting much greater from you, yet you let your standard be what others are doing. Never compare your God-given standard of faithfulness to another person's level. Instead, stay hungry as discussed in chapter 7. We choose to press ahead!

So what if you've been on five mission trips and your buddy has only been on two. If God wants you to do another, you should! Who cares if you've fostered two children and no one in your Bible study group has fostered any. If you feel Jesus leading you to welcome a third, press ahead.

Congratulations, you've faithfully served in the church for 20 years. That is a remarkable and sacrificial act that God has used to grow you and others, but don't you dare look around and begin to coast just because you've done more than people around you. Staying focused on his unique, God-given work for years helped Paul finish strong. In Philippians 3:13–14 he says:

> Brothers and sisters, I do not consider myself yet to have taken hold of it. But one thing I do: forgetting what is behind and straining toward what is ahead, I press on toward the goal to win the prize for which God has called me heavenward in Christ Jesus.

Paul never allowed his past faithfulness to distract him from his current calling. He didn't focus on doing more than those around him, but on winning the prize for finishing his race. Only when we stop focusing on all we've done and what others are doing, do we see what God wants us to do next.

This parable in Luke 18 shows that God would rather use a humble tax collector who is willing to be shaped and molded than a self-righteous Pharisee whose good works have hardened him into a complacent, arrogant and fearless man. The Pharisee felt good when comparing himself to others and was satisfied. The tax collector felt inadequate when comparing himself to his holy God and felt desperate.

If we are to compare ourselves to anyone, let it be to the perfection and example of our Savior. That comparison will humble us as we realize how distant we are from His standard of perfection. In this humility, we confess our need for Him. In this humility, we are not only justified and made right with God, but we hunger to press on toward the goal. When Jesus is our standard of holiness, we dare not compare ourselves to anyone else.

DOUBTING THAT YOU MATTER

Sometimes we compare ourselves to others and find ground to boast. That practice is bad enough, but more likely for most of us is the sad scenario that when we compare ourselves to others we don't measure up. Doubting that you matter is a dangerous result of making comparisons and it paralyzes God's people to inaction. You feel someone else is a better fit, more capable, a better leader, better prepared, so you defer to them.

Have you ever said, "I wish I knew as much as that person?" Perhaps you've thought, "If only I had the time they had, I could really accomplish something big." Or maybe you compare your finances, abilities or even your testimony to people you barely know.

As you do this, you have subtly excused yourself and sought out comfort in your own pity. Instead of doing the most you can with what you have on the task God gave you, you bury your talent and produce nothing but excuses. Comparison has killed your calling.

OFFER WHAT YOU HAVE

Luke 21 starts with Jesus revealing the heart of His Father.

> As Jesus looked up, he saw the rich putting their gifts into the temple treasury. He also saw a poor widow put in two very small copper coins. "Truly I tell you," he said, "this poor woman has put in more than all the others. All these people gave their gifts out of their wealth; but she out of her poverty put in all she had to live on."

Offer me what you have, Jesus is saying. I want nothing more. I expect nothing less. That is the heart of God. Jesus publicly declares that this poor widow, who has offered two of the smallest value coins, is demonstrating more faith and obedience than anyone because she's giving all she has. She held nothing back from the Father. Instead of comparing her meager offering to the flamboyant rich around her, she simply gave what she had—everything she had. Her offering will be rewarded for eternity as she is recognized as a "faithful servant."

Think how easy it would have been for the poor widow to consider her resources too meager and to reject God's invitation to give what she had. Listening to the gold coins others dropped loudly into the offering jar, she could have doubted that her copper bits would ever matter. Instead of waiting until maybe she had more, she trusted God to use her faithfulness now. She knew God would never demand more than she had to offer, so she decided to give Him everything.

When I read this account, I can't help but think about times I have stored up blessings that I had been entrusted to steward, invest and grow. I compare myself to another, more experienced steward and determine to wait until I reach their level of expertise before I act.

I lie to myself and say my financial contribution to God's Kingdom couldn't come close to what others can do, so I will defer and let them carry the burden. I question how my limited ability to lead could ever make a difference in the church, so I let others lead until "my time" has arrived.

As soon as my focus drops to what others have or can do instead of what is expected of me, I have failed to be faithful. In these weak moments when I am tempted to delay action until I know more theology, have more money, or develop more leadership qualities, I must remind myself that God is asking me to offer Him what I do have, now. He wants my obedience.

We must stop comparing ourselves to others and begin weighing whether or not we have offered Him all that we have.

WHAT'S THE POINT?

The widow's offering in Luke 21 isn't about money. If it was, those who gave gold coins would be the story's heroes. The point is to give all you have to God and trust that He sees it as good, no matter how insignificant it seems to you. It is about trusting that your offering, no matter how big or small, is not wasted. It is about trusting God to do His part as you do yours.

Comparison kills this trust. If we compare our offering to the enormity of what needs to be done, we could be discouraged. How easy it is to think the size of the problem is bigger than our God. Measuring our contribution against the need chokes out faithfulness. Such comparison tells us we will never be able to fix the problem, so why contribute to a false solution? There will always be more work to do, so why even get started?

Instead of playing our part as a faithful servant in this great drama, we assume the role of Master. Instead of focusing our energy on obedience, we burn it up making decisions that really are not ours to make, about whether our efforts, our gifts, our obedience are worth the sacrifice.

When comparison begins to rob you of faithfulness, let me remind you what's at stake.

To this day, I remember feeling a burden lifted from me the first time I heard someone say, "You can't do everything for everyone, but you can do something for someone." I no longer felt pressure to do it all. Instead, I found joy in the process. Maybe I couldn't change the world, but I could help change a life. Maybe my efforts would result in greater progress against the total need, but if not, I could still do *something* for *someone*!

We need to fight against comparison that leads to despair because someone's life is at stake. Reject the temptation to be dismayed by the size of the need so you can focus on the importance of the *one*. We serve a Good Shepherd who loves enough to leave His 99 sheep in the pasture and focus on the one missing, so why shouldn't we do the same? In the words of Andy Stanley, we should, "Do for one what you wish you could do for everyone."[1]

You may not be able to eliminate prescription drug abuse in your region, but you can support someone to pursue sobriety. You may not be able to care for all 153 million orphans[2] in the world, but you can find a home, be a parent, provide food and clothing for one of them. You may not find the cure for cancer, but you can choose to finish nursing school and be the hands of Jesus as you care for those suffering from it.

All these things are possible if you are faithful. None of them will happen if you focus more on what you don't have than on faithfully offering what you do. Comparison has fed our *someday* excuse for years. When we decide whether or not we have offered Jesus everything we do have—regardless of what we don't—we exchange that great mental roadblock of *someday* for the expressway of *today*. Today we do what we can, nothing more and nothing less.

ASK YOURSELF:

- To who or what have I been comparing myself? How has that kept me from being a faithful steward of what I do have?

- What is something I can do for someone today that could change his or her life?

- In what area of my life do I feel inadequate to meet the needs I see around me? Can I see how He has gifted me uniquely to meet a need that maybe only I can see?

- Is there anything I am keeping for myself instead of willingly giving over to God? How would my life be different if I gave Him everything?

CHAPTER 12
I HAVE FINISHED THE RACE

JUST KEEP RUNNING

> For I am already being poured out like a drink offering, and the time for my departure is near.⁷ I have fought the good fight, I have finished the race, I have kept the faith. ⁸ Now there is in store for me the crown of righteousness, which the Lord, the righteous Judge, will award to me on that day—and not only to me, but also to all who have longed for his appearing. (2 Timothy 4:6–8)

In the fall of 2016, I ran my first, and likely last, half-marathon. I never imagined I would pay money for the privilege of running for over two hours straight. My attitude changed when the cute girl I was dating—who eventually became my wife—kept dropping hints that she'd like to run one together. Trying to impress, I signed us up.

For the next three months we trained together for a grueling 13.1-mile race through Nashville, Tennessee. Our race day goal was simple: to run the entire route without stopping. No matter how slow or fast, I wanted to be able to say I ran 13.1 miles straight.

At the starting line, I felt like a million bucks. I don't know if you have ever competed in a race, but a certain type of energy sparkles and snaps in the air when you run with hundreds of people around you.

We started the race and felt great the first seven miles. Carried along with the crowd, our pace was quicker than we planned and I even remembered thinking, "I bet I could run a full marathon. If I continue feeling this good, I should just go for the full 26.2 miles."

We continued to push each other and enjoyed a few encouraging conversations with other runners along the way. Then it happened. Bam. We hit the wall. Somewhere between mile 8 and 9, everything changed. Muscles started screaming. Breathing became more labored. Feet began to hurt. I think my teeth even ached. The energy from race day excitement drained like an old battery and was replaced with the daunting thought of still having another 45 minutes of running ahead of us.

Our pace slowed substantially along a brutally straight and dull three-mile stretch beside the Cumberland River. "Just keep running. Whatever you do, just keep running." I repeated this mantra regularly as Madeline and I trudged forward. We slowed, but stopping was never an option.

The Apostle Paul knew what it meant to finish a race. He wrote his final letter to Timothy from jail, just days before he was martyred by the Roman government. After Jesus dramatically changed his life, Paul lived every day for the One most worthy. Was Paul perfect? Nope. Was his life of faithfulness challenging? Yep. He compared his life to a fight worth fighting.

Until taking his final breath, Paul never stopped running his race and fighting his fight. He never looked back satisfied with how far he had come. Paul knew the only thing that mattered was crossing the finish line and attaining his prize. He longed for the crown to be awarded by the righteous Judge himself. So, he never stopped running.

The word "crown" in verse eight comes from the Greek word *stephanos*. It doesn't mean a gold crown of royalty. Jesus alone wears that crown. It refers to the modest crown of olive leaves given to the victor at the end of a competition. It declares victory to all who see it atop the head of a competitor. *Stephanos* is also the name of the first Christian martyr. We know him as Stephen.

I can only imagine, as Paul writes some of his last words, that he reflects on the day he not only witnessed Stephen's stoning, but approved of it. Decades earlier Paul was an insecure, brutal, works-driven religionist who persecuted Christians. Stephen's death was a victory for him. And now, he is staring at the finish line, with just a few steps to go before he bows his head and receives his *stephanos*. He kept the faith. He finished the race.

We, too, have a *stephanos*, a crown of victory, waiting for us. Maybe like Paul you had a late start. God doesn't care! He just asks that we finish the race before us, no matter how long the journey.

Too often we run, and halfway through we question whether the reward is worth the pain. Will our next step matter? Will anyone notice, know or care if we drop out? But if we keep running, no matter how hard it is or how long the race seems, we will one day attain the prize. Not because we earned it by what we accomplished along the way. Jesus already has won the race for us. We receive the prize simply because we were faithful and we finished.

PARTICIPATION TROPHIES

Young Millennials like myself catch a lot of criticism for being given trophies just for participating. Coaches and parents don't want kids to feel bad if competition separated winners from losers and someone had to go home without a trophy. Frankly, I think it's healthy to compete and announce a winner. But, praise God, we don't earn this prize toward which we run, the crown of righteousness, by running harder or faster. We receive it because we take the next step and the next step until we cross the line.

Jesus became the victor when he overcame the grave and he awaits our finish on the podium. Paul now knows his race is just one of personal faithfulness. His focus is no longer on being perfect or earning God's favor or being more fervent than the person next to him. He now just wants to take his next step until he finishes.

As Madeline and I struggled through the final few miles of our race in Nashville, we were somewhere around 400th place. We had no chance at winning, as hundreds had already finished. But that didn't stop us from running the best race we could. I understood that I didn't have to run the fastest race to receive my reward. Waiting for me was a participation medal and the satisfaction of knowing I ran 13.1 miles without stopping. As long as I just kept taking next steps, my prize was secure. Because of that, we could keep running.

Where are you in your race? Maybe you haven't even started because it seems too daunting. Before I met Madeline, I never imagined running 13 miles straight. Even considering that distance seemed like a joke to me. For many people, a life of faithfully following Jesus just seems too difficult even to attempt.

Others jump off to a blazing start, hit full stride quickly and maintain it through a long and faithful life. They hunger to do the work of the Father more than anything in their lives.

And then there are those who are starting to coast. You planned your race, started at a good pace and maintained it for a while. But now you find yourself slowing down and struggling to continue. Each step is harder and you begin to covet the old times when the race was easier.

You reflect on the times when you would read God's word for hours and were moved to tears during worship as you felt the Spirit moving in your heart. You recall the years when you were a critical part of a growing church or you started a new ministry to reach the lost and the least. You look back to the days when you got to baptize others and saw life change all around you.

For a moment, these memories fuel a surge of energy, until suddenly you realize that it's been years since you've experienced any of those joys. Sadness sets in.

You continue to struggle onward but now the question rings through your head, "Why is my faith so stale?" You ask God why you haven't heard from Him. You wonder why scripture seems so dead if it's supposed to be alive and active. Bitterness grips your heart as you realize you can't remember the last time you got "that feeling" in worship service.

During these parts of our race, where each step seems more impossible than the last, it's easy to start blaming everyone but ourselves. The pastor's preaching doesn't ring the bell anymore. The worship team isn't picking songs that engage me. My Bible study teacher isn't preparing well. As we draw more inward we say our community isn't reaching out. We even blame God for forgetting us. The excuses are endless.

As much as we would like to point the finger elsewhere when our faith grows stale, the honest truth is that it's all you. You've slowed down, compared yourself to others and feel you've "done enough." You no longer take risks or embrace the joys of sacrifice. You're proud of how far you've come, instead of pressing humbly toward what's ahead.

Living in the past is a terrible way to run your current race. Looking to experience God in old ways and expecting Him to repeat Himself will lead to disappointment. Instead of striding ahead, you jog in place. God wants you to trust Him to take steps into something new! Even though you feel this pull to take next steps, you wait for *someday* because the comfort of recreating what you've already experienced has won you over.

Have you forgotten that you serve a God who redeems and is making all things new? Don't neglect God's call to take new steps to experience Him in new ways.

God's pace is perfect. Sometimes He will have you sprint into something new. Other times He will slow you down to allow for recovery. One thing is sure: He will always draw you into something fresh and different. When the race becomes difficult, when you're tired, when the path is boring and the hills are steep, just keep your feet moving. Taking seasons to slow down is sometimes wise.

But whatever you do, don't stop taking steps. And don't ever let the thought of *someday* doing something great deceive you into thinking you are making progress. You haven't accomplished anything until you choose to make *someday* today.

THE END IS IN SIGHT

Just as Madeline and I were tempted to throw in the towel toward the end of that endless 3-mile stretch, the route brought us back into downtown Nashville. For the last mile or so we traded the straight and bland riverside view for twists, turns and tourists, whose energy we absorbed. Amazingly, mile 13 was one of my favorite miles of the race.

As I approached the finish line I realized a truth that still sticks with me. Sometimes we expect God to pour joy and excitement into our lives with every step we take. We create pressure for each step to be more exciting than the last. In reality, some parts of the race just aren't that compelling.

There will be stretches that require you to just put your head down and push through until you reach a more enjoyable place to run. In these moments, we trust that our diligence is worth the price! Why? Because running the race in the ordinary times positions you to experience the extraordinary.

Sometimes you have to plod through the mundane stretch where the landscape never seems to change before you realize all that God has accomplished and brought you through. It's faithfulness in the ordinary days when each step mirrors the last, that leads you towards the end and into something new.

If there is one thing you glean from this book, let it be this: Following Jesus is not about performing. We must give up that idea! Following Jesus is about walking with Him, one step at a time, trusting He is good enough so you don't have to compete. It is about believing deeply that He is so good, you will do whatever is required to take your next step with Him into something new. You realize the sacrifice required to lift your heavy foot into that step pales in comparison to the joy of running with our Creator into the new thing He has for you.

It took me about 25,000 steps to reach the finish line that morning in Nashville. Some steps were easy, others miserable. Either way, I had to take every one of them. Although I don't plan on doing it again, the satisfaction I experienced knowing I did not stop, made running the race worth it.

That morning as I crossed the finish line I tasted a hint of the satisfaction that awaits me if I can finish well this bigger race of life. While I still have millions of steps to take, I know my God is enough and will be with me the entire time.

I want to encourage you to really spend some time on this last "Ask Yourself" section. Spend a few days or weeks being honest and wrestling with these questions. As you do, remember this one final truth:

Jesus finished His race to give you a race worth running. Every step He took towards Calvary, He took with you in mind. Every painful breath He drew while stretched on the cross, He did so purposefully until He could exclaim, "It is finished." He refused to stay in the tomb because His race continued until He took away the sting of death.

We run our race toward Jesus, in anticipation of Jesus, and because of Jesus. Because Jesus finished His race, we can run ours, knowing we have a prize in store. And that prize is Christ Himself.

He is enough.

ASK YOURSELF:

- Right now, what is my next step? What is the step I have put off for *someday* that I need to take today?

- What needs to stop or start today so that I can get one step closer to finishing my race?

- How will I allow God's goodness to carry me into unthinkable and unimaginable steps of faith?

- Do I truly believe God is enough when I am not? If I don't believe it, confess that to Him and ask for more faith. If I do believe it, pick a God-sized dream and begin taking steps towards it right now.

- Your *Someday* starts today.

ACKNOWLEDGEMENTS

Starting a book at twenty-four years old is a daunting task that is only possible with an amazing team supporting you every step of the way. The most important aspect of life is having people who will always point you back to the sufficiency of Christ. Thank you to everyone who has helped me realize I am enough because Jesus is enough.

To North Ridge Community Church- Thank you for always seeing me as Jesus sees me. None of this journey would be possible without you. You have trusted me to lead through influence at an age that many would write off. Thank you for the constant support, encouragement, opportunities, and love. Let's keep going until our entire region is transformed by the power of Jesus!

To my wife, Madeline- You are my ultimate example of the unconditional love of Christ. I have the courage to step into the unknown because I know you will be with me every step of the way. Thank you for giving me courage through love.

To my family- You have never stopped believing in me. Thank you for always seeing who I can be, not just who I am. Because of that, Jesus continues to change my life.

To Hannah Samsel and Sam Scott- You have blessed so many through helping make this book possible. Thank you for not only editing this book, but walking with me through this journey.

To my text editor, Norman Jameson- You have helped make this book come alive! Thank you for using your unique gift to serve Him in a profound way.

To Jesus- You are everything. The only reason this book exists is because you are enough. I love you so much.

NOTES

Chapter 2
1   Guzik, David. "Study Guide for Jeremiah 1." Blue Letter Bible. 2013. Accessed August 1, 2018.

Chapter 3
1   Guzik, David. "Study Guide for James 1." Blue Letter Bible. 2013. Accessed August 1, 2018. https://www.blueletterbible.org/Comm/guzik_david/StudyGuide2017-Jam/Jam-1.cfm.
2   Mineo, Andy. *1:The Arrow-Clarity*. Reach Records/Miner League, 2018. [Online]. [Accessed 7 Sep. 2018].
3   Charles Spurgeon. *Spurgeon's Sermons Volume 50:* 1904
4   Anderson, Matthew Lee. *The End of Our Exploring: A Book about Questioning and the Confidence of Faith*. Chicago: Moody Publishers, 2013.
5   Vanderstelt, Jeff. *Gospel Fluency: Speaking the Truths of Jesus into the Everyday Stuff of Life*. Wheaton, IL: Crossway, 2017.

Chapter 4
1   Norton, Ken, Joe Frazier, Marshall Terrill, and Mike Fitzgerald. Going the Distance. Champaign, IL: Sports Pub., 2000.
2   Sullivan, Erin M., MPH. "Suicide Trends Among Persons Aged 10–24 Years - United States, 1994–2012." Centers for Disease Control and Prevention. March 06, 2015. Accessed October 15, 2018. https://www.cdc.gov/mmwr/preview/mmwrhtml/mm6408a1.htm.

Chapter 5
1   Shipnuck, Alan, Tom Verducci, Steve Rushin, L. Jon Wertheim, Michael Rosenberg, David Kahn, Robert Klemko, Jeremy Fuchs, and Kelsey

Mckinney. "The Case for ... Monica Abbott." SI.com. June 26, 2017. Accessed September 27, 2018. https://www.si.com/vault/2017/06/20/case-monica-abbott.

2   New World Encyclopedia Contributors. "George B. McClellan." Ohio River - New World Encyclopedia. Accessed September 26, 2018. http://www.newworldencyclopedia.org/p/index.php?title=George_B._McClellan&oldid=1005124.

3   New World Encyclopedia Contributors. "Ulysses S. Grant." Ohio River - New World Encyclopedia. Accessed September 26, 2018. http://www.newworldencyclopedia.org/p/index.php?title=Ulysses_S._Grant&oldid=977511.

Chapter 6

1   Drake. Future. What A Time To Be. Cash Money Records, 2015. [Online]. [Accessed 7 Sep. 2018].

2   Maxwell, John C. *The 21 Irrefutable Laws of Leadership: Follow Them and People Will Follow You*. Nashville, TN: Thomas Nelson.

3   Shellnutt, Kate, Sarah Eekhoff Zylstra, Jeremy Weber, Matthew Sleeth, and Jayson Casper. "Here's How America Is Praising Its Best-Known Preacher: Billy Graham." Christian History | Learn the History of Christianity & the Church. Accessed September 27, 2018. https://www.christianitytoday.com/news/2018/february/how-america-is-praising-evangelist-billy-graham-tribute.html.

Chapter 7

1   Lewis, C. S. The Weight of Glory and Other Addresses. London: William Collins, 2013.

2   Acuff, Jon. *FINISH: Give Yourself the Gift of Done*. S.l.: Portfolio Penguin, 2018.

Chapter 8

1   Giglio, Louie. The Comeback. Place of Publication Not Identified: Thomas Nelson Pub, 2015.

2   Buster, Bobette. *DO STORY: How To Tell Your Story So The World Listens*. DO BOOK, 2018.

3   Story, Laura. "Your Painful Story Brings God Glory." Desiring God. November 1, 2015. Accessed September 27, 2018. https://www.desiringgod.org/articles/your-painful-story-brings-god-glory.

Chapter 9

1. Elevation Worship. There Is A Cloud. "There Is A Cloud". Provident Label Group, 2017. [Online]. [Accessed 7 Sep. 2018].
2. Todd, Michael. *"Before the Person :: Relationship Goals (Part 1)"* Sermon, #Relationship Goal, Tulsa, Oklahoma, August 6, 2017.
3. Letter from John Newton. August 19th, 1775. London, England
4. "V Foundation for Cancer Research | Victory Over Cancer." V Foundation. Accessed September 28, 2018. https://www.jimmyv.org/.

Chapter 10

1. Guzik, David. "Study Guide for Matthew 25." Blue Letter Bible. 2013. Accessed November 1, 2018. https://www.blueletterbible.org/Comm/guzik_david/StudyGuide2017-Mat/Mat-25.cfm

Chapter 11

1. Woodley, Matt. "Catalyst 2011 Andy Stanley: Be Present." Christian History | Learn the History of Christianity & the Church. October 2011. Accessed September 28, 2018. https://www.christianitytoday.com/pastors/2011/october-online-only/catalyst-2011-andy-stanley-be-present.html.
2. "Christian Alliance for Orphans White Paper On Understanding Orphan Statistics." Accessed November 2, 2018. https://cafo.org/wp-content/uploads/2017/10/Orphan-Statistics-Web-06.2018.pdf.

CPSIA information can be obtained
at www.ICGtesting.com
Printed in the USA
LVHW040129020319
609286LV00001B/42